GRADE 8

P9-AGN-953

MATH Trailblazers®

A BALANCED MATHEMATICS PROGRAM INTEGRATING SCIENCE AND LANGUAGE ARTS

Unit Resource Guide
Unit 16
Volume

THIRD EDITION

KENDALL/HUNT PUBLISHING COMPANY
4050 Westmark Drive   Dubuque, Iowa 52002

A TIMS® Curriculum
University of Illinois at Chicago

UIC The University of Illinois
at Chicago

The original edition was based on work supported by the National Science Foundation under grant
No. MDR 9050226 and the University of Illinois at Chicago. Any opinions, findings, and conclusions
or recommendations expressed in this publication are those of the author(s) and do not necessarily
reflect the views of the granting agencies.

Copyright © 1997, 2004, 2008 by Kendall/Hunt Publishing Company

ISBN 978-0-7575-3591-8

All rights reserved. No part of this publication may be reproduced, stored in a retrieval system,
or transmitted, in any form or by any means, electronic, mechanical, photocopying, recording, or
otherwise, without the prior written permission of the copyright owner. Permission is granted to the
purchaser to reproduce each blackline master in quantities suitable for non-commercial classroom use.

Printed in the United States of America

1 2 3 4 5 6 7 8 9 10   11 10 09 08 07

Letter Home

Volume

Date: _____

Dear Family Member:

In this math unit, we are studying volume, which is a measurement of size. It is the amount of space an object takes up. If the volume is a container, such as a box or a jar, then it is the amount of space inside. In this unit, students will explore ways to find volumes of both solid objects and containers.

First, students estimate the volumes of small objects by making models from centimeter cubes. Then they measure the volume of these objects by displacement, putting them under water in a graduated cylinder and measuring how much the water rises. In the lab *Fill 'er Up!,* they measure the volume of containers by pouring graduated cylinders full of water into the containers and using addition and subtraction to find the total volume. They also use their data to solve problems involving multiplication and division.

In the metric system, volume is measured in liters, milliliters, and cubic centimeters (1 milliliter = 1 cubic centimeter). In the U.S. Customary system, common units include the gallon, quart, and cubic inch. Most of our measurements in class are in cubic centimeters.

The rock made the water rise from 50 to 63 cubic centimeters.

That means the volume of the rock is 13 cubic centimeters.

- In a homework activity, *Volume Hunt,* we ask you to help your child find containers that hold cups, pints, quarts, or gallons.

- Help your child review the multiplication facts for the 2s, 5s, and 10s using the *Triangle Flash Cards.*

Measuring volume by displacement

Thank you for your continuing support at home of our mathematics work.

Sincerely,

_____

Copyright © Kendall/Hunt Publishing Company

Carta al hogar

Volumen

Fecha: _____

Estimado miembro de familia:

En esta unidad, estudiaremos el volumen, que es una medida del tamaño. Es la cantidad de espacio que ocupa un objeto. Si se trata del volumen de un recipiente, como una caja o una jarra, entonces se refiere a la cantidad de espacio que hay dentro. En esta unidad, los estudiantes explorarán maneras de hallar el volumen tanto de objetos sólidos como de recipientes.

En primer lugar, los estudiantes estiman los volúmenes de objetos pequeños haciendo modelos con cubos de un centímetro. Luego miden el volumen de estos objetos por desplazamiento, colocándolos en el agua en un cilindro graduado y midiendo cuánto aumenta el nivel de agua. En la investigación llamada *¡Llénalo!,* los estudiantes medirán el volumen de recipientes vertiendo en ellos agua de cilindros graduados y usando la suma y la resta para hallar el volumen total. También usarán sus datos para resolver problemas que requieren el uso de la multiplicación y la división.

Medir el volumen por desplazamiento

En el sistema métrico, el volumen se mide en litros, mililitros y centímetros cúbicos (1 mililitro = 1 centímetro cúbico). En el sistema estadounidense, las unidades comunes incluyen el galón, el cuarto de galón y la pulgada cúbica. La mayoría de las mediciones hechas en clase son en centímetros cúbicos.

- En una actividad para el hogar llamada *Caza de volúmenes,* le pedimos que ayude a su hijo/a a encontrar recipientes que tengan una capacidad de una taza, una pinta, un cuarto de galón o un galón.

- Ayude a su hijo/a a repasar las tablas de multiplicación del 2, el 5 y el 10 usando las tarjetas triangulares.

Gracias por su continuo apoyo en casa de nuestro trabajo de matemáticas.

Atentamente,

_____

Copyright © Kendall/Hunt Publishing Company

Table of Contents

Unit 16
Volume

Unit 16

Outline
Volume

Unit Summary

Estimated Class Sessions
6-7

To begin the unit, students estimate the volume of small objects by building models with centimeter connecting cubes. They then check their estimates using a graduated cylinder and measuring the volume of the objects by displacement. In the lab *Fill 'er Up!*, students measure the volume of several containers, record the measurements in a data table, and graph the results. They use the data to predict how many of one container will be needed to fill another. This provides a context for investigating division with remainders and solving problems involving multiplication. In the Adventure Book, *Elixir of Youth,* two investigators use their volume skills when the liquid inside an ancient jar is stolen from a museum's collection. Students also discover the relationships between U.S. Customary units of measuring volume—the cup, pint, quart, and gallon. The DPP for this unit practices and assesses the multiplication facts for the twos, fives, and tens.

Major Concept Focus

- estimating volume in cubic centimeters
- capacity
- measuring volume with graduated cylinders
- measuring volume in metric and customary units
- TIMS Laboratory Method
- *Adventure Book:* finding the volume of a container
- bar graphs
- scales
- number sentences
- multiplication as repeated addition
- multidigit addition and subtraction
- division as repeated subtraction
- predicting
- practice and assessment of the multiplication facts for the 2s, 5s, and 10s
- checking predictions

Pacing Suggestions

- Lesson 1 *Measuring Volume* and Lesson 2 *Fill 'er Up!* connect strongly to science. In Lesson 1 students measure volume by counting cubic centimeters and using graduated cylinders. Lesson 2 is a lab that uses science-process skills to investigate the volume of containers. Use science time to complete portions of these lessons.

- Lesson 4 *Elixir of Youth* connects to both social studies and language arts. Students can read the story during either of these classes.

Assessment Indicators

Use the following Assessment Indicators and the *Observational Assessment Record* that follows the Background section in this unit to assess students on key ideas.

A1. Can students measure volume using a graduated cylinder?

A2. Can students collect, organize, graph, and analyze data?

A3. Can students make and interpret bar graphs?

A4. Can students solve addition, subtraction, multiplication, and division problems involving volume?

A5. Do students demonstrate fluency with the multiplication facts for the 2s, 5s, and 10s?

Unit Planner

KEY: SG = Student Guide, DAB = Discovery Assignment Book, AB = Adventure Book, URG = Unit Resource Guide, DPP = Daily Practice and Problems, HP = Home Practice (found in Discovery Assignment Book), and TIG = Teacher Implementation Guide.

	Lesson Information	Supplies	Copies/Transparencies
Lesson 1 **Measuring Volume** URG Pages 19–37 SG Pages 236–243 DPP A–B HP Part 1 *Estimated Class Sessions* **1**	**Activity** Students find the volume of various solid objects. First, they estimate the volume by making a model from centimeter connecting cubes. Then they measure the volume by placing the object inside a graduated cylinder and determining the amount of water that it displaces. **Homework** 1. Assign the Homework section on the *Measuring Volume* Activity Pages. 2. Assign Part 1 of the Home Practice. **Assessment** Use the *Observational Assessment Record* to note students' abilities to measure volume by displacement.	• small solid objects that fit inside a graduated cylinder • 1 graduated cylinder calibrated no more than 2 cc apart and large enough to hold small objects (250 cc preferred) per student group • 1 eyedropper per student group • 1 beaker or container of water per student group • 2 handfuls of centimeter connecting cubes per student group • several sheets of paper towels per student group • 1 centimeter ruler per student	• 1 copy of *Three-column Data Table* URG Page 34 per student • 1 transparency of *Scale 1 with Blowup* URG Page 30 • 1 transparency of *Scale 2 with Blowup* URG Page 31 • 1 transparency of *Scale 3 with Blowup* URG Page 32 • 1 transparency of *Meniscus* URG Page 33 • 1 copy of *Observational Assessment Record* URG Pages 9–10 to be used throughout this unit
Lesson 2 **Fill 'er Up!** URG Pages 38–59 SG Pages 244–248 DPP C–H HP Parts 2–3 *Estimated Class Sessions* **3**	**Lab** Students find the volume of various containers by pouring graduated cylinders of water into each container (or vice versa) and using addition and subtraction to calculate the total volume. Students use the data to solve problems involving multiplication and division. **Math Facts** DPP Bits C, E, and G provide practice with multiplication facts for the 2s, 5s, and 10s. **Homework** 1. For homework students finish questions not completed in class. 2. Assign Parts 2 and 3 of the Home Practice. 3. Students continue to practice the multiplication facts for the 2s, 5s, and 10s using their *Triangle Flash Cards*. 4. Assign *Questions 1–2* on the *Volume Hunt* Activity Pages for Lesson 3 in the *Discovery Assignment Book*. **Assessment** 1. Use *Questions 10–11* on the *Fill 'er Up!* Lab Pages to assess students' understanding of how to measure volume. 2. Assign scores to one or more parts of the lab. 3. Use the *Observational Assessment Record* to note students' abilities to collect, organize, graph, and analyze data. 4. Use DPP Task F Volume as a quiz.	• 1 small, 1 medium, and 1 large container per student group • 1 250 cc graduated cylinder per student group • 1 eyedropper per student group • paper towels • 1 large irregular-shaped jar • 1 cup or small container per student group • 1 dishpan container per student group	• 1 copy of *Centimeter Graph Paper* URG Page 51 per student • 1 copy of *Three-trial Data Table* URG Page 52 per student, optional • 1 copy of *Triangle Flash Cards 2s, 5s,* and *10s* URG Pages 53–55 per student, optional

	Lesson Information	**Supplies**	**Copies/ Transparencies**

Lesson 3

Volume Hunt

URG Pages 60–67
DAB Pages 247–248

DPP I–J
HP Part 4

Estimated Class Sessions
1

Activity
Students search at home for containers whose volume is measured in U.S. Customary Units: cup, pint, quart, and gallon. Activities at home and at school develop the relationships between these units of measurement.

Math Facts
Task J provides practice with multiplication facts and money.

Homework
1. *Questions 1–2* of the *Volume Hunt* Activity Pages were assigned at the end of Lesson 2.
2. Assign Part 4 of the Home Practice.

Assessment
Use the *Observational Assessment Record* to document students' abilities to solve addition, subtraction, multiplication, and division problems involving volume.

• 1 dishpan or large container per student group
• paper towels
• 2 containers of different sizes at home: cup, pint, quart, or gallon per student and 1 each for the teacher

• 1 transparency of *Volume Hunt* data table DAB Page 248, optional

Lesson 4

Elixir of Youth

URG Pages 68–76
AB Pages 95–114

DPP K–L

Estimated Class Sessions
1

Adventure Book
Sam V. and Tess V. Shovel, ace volume investigators, are on a case at the Oriental Museum. Someone has stolen the liquid contents of an ancient jar in the museum's collection, and Tess and Sam must use their volume skills to solve the mystery.

Math Facts
DPP Bit K is a multiplication quiz on the 2s, 5s, and 10s.

Homework
Assign the word problems in Lesson 5.

Assessment
1. Use DPP Bit K to assess students on the multiplication facts for the 2s, 5s, and 10s.
2. Use DPP Task L to assess students on measuring volume by displacement.
3. Use the *Observational Assessment Record* to note students' abilities to use addition, subtraction, multiplication, and division to solve volume problems.
4. Transfer appropriate documentation from the *Observational Assessment Record* to students' *Individual Assessment Record Sheets*.

• map of the Middle East, optional

• 1 copy of *Individual Assessment Record Sheet* TIG Assessment section per student, previously copied for use throughout the year

(Continued)

	Lesson Information	Supplies	Copies/ Transparencies
Lesson 5 **Paying Taxes Problems** URG Pages 77–79 SG Page 249 *Estimated Class Sessions* **1**	OPTIONAL LESSON **Optional Activity** As a follow-up to Unit 15 *Decimal Investigations,* students solve problems involving money. **Homework** Assign some or all of the problems for homework.		

Connections

A current list of literature and software connections is available at *www.mathtrailblazers.com.* You can also find information on connections in the *Teacher Implementation Guide* Literature List and Software List sections.

Literature Connections

Suggested Titles

- Adler, David. *How Tall, How Short, How Far Away.* Holiday House, New York, 2000.
- Brown, Stephanie Gwyn. *Aesop's The Crow and The Pitcher.* Tricycle Press, Berkeley, CA, 2003.
- Schwartz, David M. *Millions to Measure.* Harper Trophy, New York, 2006.

Software Connections

- *Building Perspective Deluxe* develops spatial reasoning and visual thinking in three dimensions.
- Graphers is a data graphing tool appropriate for young students.
- *Kid Pix* allows students to create their own illustrations.

Teaching All Math Trailblazers Students

Math Trailblazers® lessons are designed for students with a wide range of abilities. The lessons are flexible and do not require significant adaptation for diverse learning styles or academic levels. However, when needed, lessons can be tailored to allow students to engage their abilities to the greatest extent possible while building knowledge and skills.

To assist you in meeting the needs of all students in your classroom, this section contains information about some of the features in the curriculum that allow all students access to mathematics. For additional information, see the Teaching the *Math Trailblazers* Student: Meeting Individual Needs section in the *Teacher Implementation Guide*.

Differentiation Opportunities in this Unit

Laboratory Experiments

Laboratory experiments enable students to solve problems using a variety of representations including pictures, tables, graphs, and symbols. Teachers can assign or adapt parts of the analysis according to the student's ability. The following lesson is a lab:

- Lesson 2 *Fill 'er Up!*

Journal Prompts

Journal prompts provide opportunities for students to explain and reflect on mathematical problems. They can help both students who need practice explaining their ideas and students who benefit from answering higher order questions. Students with various learning styles can express themselves using pictures, words, and sentences. Teachers can alter journal prompts to suit students' ability levels. The following lessons contain a journal prompt:

- Lesson 1 *Measuring Volume*
- Lesson 2 *Fill 'er Up!*
- Lesson 4 *Elixir of Youth*

DPP Challenges

DPP Challenges are items from the Daily Practice and Problems that usually take more than fifteen minutes to complete. These problems are more thought-provoking and can be used to stretch students' problem-solving skills. The following lesson has a DPP Challenge in it:

- DPP Challenge B from Lesson 1 *Measuring Volume*

Extensions

Use extensions to enrich lessons. Many extensions provide opportunities to further involve or challenge students of all abilities. Take a moment to review the extensions prior to beginning this unit. Some extensions may require additional preparation and planning. The following lessons contain extensions:

- Lesson 1 *Measuring Volume*
- Lesson 2 *Fill 'er Up!*
- Lesson 3 *Volume Hunt*
- Lesson 4 *Elixir of Youth*

Background
Volume

In the activities and lab in this unit students use graduated cylinders and water to measure the volume of solid objects and of containers. First they find the volume of small solid objects by submerging them in the water in a graduated cylinder and measuring the amount of water that is displaced. This procedure, called **measuring volume by displacement,** will be familiar to students who used the *Math Trailblazers* curriculum in second grade. Then in the lab *Fill 'er Up!* children measure the volume of containers by pouring graduated cylinders of water into the containers and using arithmetic operations to determine the total volume of the container. This procedure will be new for most students.

The **volume** of a solid object, such as a rock, is the amount of space the object occupies. The **volume** of a container, such as a bottle or a jar, is the amount of space inside. The latter concept of volume is sometimes referred to as **capacity.** Usually we will use the term *volume* for both concepts since the intended meaning is clear from the context.

In this unit, students progress from using a centimeter as a unit of length and a square centimeter as a unit of area to using a cubic centimeter as a unit of volume. **A cubic centimeter (cc)** is the volume of a cube whose edges each have a length of 1 centimeter.

Students may be familiar with a larger metric unit of volume, the liter, since many beverages are sold in 1- and 2-liter bottles. A **liter (l)** is 1000 cubic centimeters. Another unit of volume frequently seen on graduated cylinders is the **milliliter (ml).** Since "milli" is a prefix that means "thousandth," a liter is also 1000 milliliters. Therefore, converting between milliliters and cubic centimeters is simple:

$$1 \text{ milliliter} = 1 \text{ cubic centimeter}$$
$$1 \text{ ml} = 1 \text{ cc}$$

More information on volume is in the TIMS Tutor: *The Concept of Volume.*

Observational Assessment Record

A1 Can students measure volume using a graduated cylinder?

A2 Can students collect, organize, graph, and analyze data?

A3 Can students make and interpret bar graphs?

A4 Can students solve addition, subtraction, multiplication, and division problems involving volume?

A5 Do students demonstrate fluency with the multiplication facts for the 2s, 5s, and 10s?

A6 _____

Name	A1	A2	A3	A4	A5	A6	Comments
1.							
2.							
3.							
4.							
5.							
6.							
7.							
8.							
9.							
10.							
11.							
12.							
13.							

Name	A1	A2	A3	A4	A5	A6	Comments
14.							
15.							
16.							
17.							
18.							
19.							
20.							
21.							
22.							
23.							
24.							
25.							
26.							
27.							
28.							
29.							
30.							
31.							
32.							

Unit 16

Daily Practice and Problems
Volume

A DPP Menu for Unit 16

Two Daily Practice and Problems (DPP) items are included for each class session listed in the Unit Outline. A scope and sequence chart for the DPP is in the *Teacher Implementation Guide*.

Icons in the Teacher Notes column designate the subject matter of each DPP item. The first item in each class session is always a Bit and the second is either a Task or Challenge. Each item falls into one or more of the categories listed below. A menu of the DPP items for Unit 16 follows.

N Number Sense A–C, E, G, I	⊠ Computation B, D, H, L	🕐 Time	⬡ Geometry F
Math Facts C, E, G, J, K	$ Money D, J	⊓ Measurement F, I, L	⊿ Data

Practicing and Assessing the Multiplication Facts

By the end of third grade, students are expected to demonstrate fluency with the multiplication facts. Through Units 3–10, students explored patterns in multiplication and developed strategies for learning the multiplication facts. In Unit 11, they began the systematic, strategies-based study of these facts. In Unit 16, students review and practice the multiplication facts for the twos, fives, and tens. The *Triangle Flash Cards* for these groups were distributed in Units 11 and 12 in the *Discovery* *Assignment Book* immediately following the Home Practice. They are also in Lesson 2. In Unit 16, DPP items C, E, G, and J provide practice with multiplication facts for these groups. Bit K is the Multiplication Quiz: 2s, 5s, 10s.

For information on the distribution and study of the multiplication facts in Grade 3, see the DPP Guide for Units 3 and 11. For a detailed explanation of our approach to learning and assessing the math facts in Grade 3, see the *Grade 3 Facts Resource Guide* and for information for Grades K–5, see the TIMS Tutor: *Math Facts* in the *Teacher Implementation Guide*.

Students may solve the items individually, in groups, or as a class. The items may also be assigned for homework. The DPPs are also available on the Teacher Resource CD.

Student Questions	Teacher Notes
Counting by 0.1s	**TIMS Bit**

Counting by 0.1s

Use your calculator to count by 0.1s starting at any number. Then try these problems.

1. Count by 0.1s to 2. Say the numbers quietly to yourself. Write down the numbers.

2. Count by 0.1s from 9 to 11. Say the numbers quietly to yourself. Write down the numbers.

TIMS Bit

Remind students how to read decimals; 9.1 is read "nine and one-tenth."

Help students use the calculator to count by 0.1s.

1. Many calculators have a constant feature. Each time you press =, the constant number and operation are repeated. Keystrokes: 0.1 + 0.1 = = = = etc. 0.1, 0.2, 0.3, 0.4, 0.5, 0.6, 0.7, 0.8, 0.9, 1, 1.1, etc. Show students the use of commas in lists of numbers.

2. Keystrokes: 9 + 0.1 = = = = etc. 9, 9.1, 9.2, 9.3, etc.

B **Decimal Missing Links**

Copy each list of numbers below. Find the missing numbers. You may use a calculator.

A. 0.1, 0.2, _____, _____, _____, 0.6

B. 0.7, 0.8, _____, _____, _____, 1.2

C. 9.6, 9.7, 9.8, _____, _____, _____, 10.2

D. 1.5, 2, 2.5, 3, _____, _____, _____, 5

E. 0.3, 0.6, 0.9, _____, _____, _____, 2.1

Make up a problem or two of your own. Trade problems with a friend. Check your friend's work.

TIMS Challenge

Linking these decimals to money may help students identify the pattern. For Question A: 0.1 is just like $.10. 9.6 is like $9.60. Ten cents is being added each time. Keystrokes: 0.1 + 0.1 = = = =

Trial and error on a calculator may help as well. For Question C: Press: 9.6 + 1 = 10.6. Too big. 9.6 + 0.5 = 10.1. Too big. 9.6 + 0.1 = 9.7, so 0.1 is being added repeatedly.

Here are the missing numbers:

A. 0.3, 0.4, 0.5

B. 0.9, 1, 1.1

C. 9.9, 10, 10.1

D. 3.5, 4, 4.5

E. 1.2, 1.5, 1.8

C **Doubles**

A. $2 \times 6 =$ B. $12 + 12 =$

C. $4 \times 6 =$ D. $2 \times 5 =$

E. $10 + 10 =$ F. $4 \times 5 =$

G. $2 \times 10 =$ H. $20 + 20 =$

I. $4 \times 10 =$

What patterns do you see? Describe a strategy for multiplying a number by 4.

TIMS Bit

One strategy for multiplying a number by 4 is to multiply first by 2. Then double the answer. These problems are designed to help students see this pattern. Ask students if they have other patterns for finding the answers to these fact problems.

Remind students to take home their *Triangle Flash Cards: 2s, 5s, and 10s* to practice the multiplication facts for these groups. Tell them when you will give the Multiplication Quiz: 2s, 5s, and 10s.

Walk-a-thon

The following are the results of a walk-a-thon.

Second Grade	Third Grade
Room 100 $214	Room 200 $147
Room 101 $161	Room 201 $262

1. How much did the Second Grade raise?

2. How much did the Third Grade raise?

3. Which grade came closer to the goal of $450?

4. How much more did Room 201 raise than Room 200?

TIMS Task

Have students solve the problems twice, using different methods: pencil and paper, calculator, or base-ten pieces.

1. $375

2. $409

3. Third Grade

4. $115

 Multiplication Patterns

A. $1 \times 5 =$ $2 \times 5 =$ $3 \times 5 =$

$4 \times 5 =$ $5 \times 5 =$ $6 \times 5 =$

$7 \times 5 =$ $8 \times 5 =$ $9 \times 5 =$

$10 \times 5 =$

B. $1 \times 10 =$ $2 \times 10 =$ $3 \times 10 =$

$4 \times 10 =$ $5 \times 10 =$ $6 \times 10 =$

$7 \times 10 =$ $8 \times 10 =$ $9 \times 10 =$

$10 \times 10 =$

What patterns do you see in both sets of problems?

TIMS Bit

A. The multiples of five are the same numbers found skip counting by fives. An even number multiplied by 5 ends in zero. An odd number multiplied by 5 ends in five.

B. The multiples of ten are the numbers found skip counting by tens. All multiples of ten end in zero. When a number is multiplied by ten, the answer is that number with a zero added to the end.

F Volume

This is 1 cubic centimeter:

1. What is the volume of each of the following shapes?

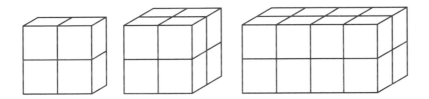

2. For each of the shapes above, use connecting cubes to build a different shape with the same volume.

TIMS Task

Have students build the shapes with cubes.

1. 4 cubic centimeters, 8 cubic centimeters, 16 cubic centimeters.

2. Answers will vary. Examples:

G More Doubles

A. $3 \times 7 =$

B. $21 + 21 =$

C. $6 \times 7 =$

D. $3 \times 8 =$

E. $24 + 24 =$

F. $6 \times 8 =$

G. $3 \times 10 =$

H. $30 + 30 =$

I. $6 \times 10 =$

What patterns do you see? Describe a strategy for multiplying a number by 6.

TIMS Bit

One strategy for multiplying a number by 6 is to multiply first by 3. Then, double the answer. These problems are designed to help students see this pattern. Ask students if they have other patterns for finding the answers to these fact problems.

Messy Student

A messy student spilled some ink on a math paper. These problems have ink on them. Can you figure out what is covered up?

1. ¹
    56
    +
    ———
    91

2. ¹
    ●3
    + 2●
    ———
    80

3. 3
    +●
    ———
    72

1. 35

2. 53 + 27

3. Answers will vary. Possible answers include:
   31 + 41; 32 + 40;
   33 + 39; 34 + 38;
   35 + 37; 36 + 36;
   37 + 35; 38 + 34;
   39 + 33

I **Missing Decimal**

Find the missing length. Write a number sentence for this problem.

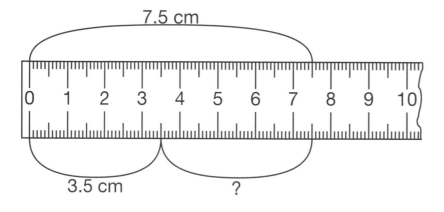

TIMS Bit

4 cm. A possible number sentence is 3.5 cm + 4 cm = 7.5 cm

Student Questions	Teacher Notes

 Mother's Helpers

TIMS Task

1. After school, Jan helps her neighbor with her new baby and earns 2 dollars each day. How much does Jan earn if she helps 4 days? 9 days? 7 days? 3 days?

2. Tony helps by going to the store for the neighbor and earns 50 cents each time. How much will Tony earn if he goes to the store 4 times? 5 times? 8 times? 9 times? Write the number sentences.

1. 8 dollars

   18 dollars

   14 dollars

   6 dollars

2. 2 dollars;
   4×50 cents = 200¢ or $2

   $2.50; 5×50¢ = $2.50

   $4.00; 8×50 cents = 400¢ or $4

   $4.50; 9×50 cents = 450¢ or $4.50

 Multiplication Quiz: 2s, 5s, and 10s

TIMS Bit

We recommend 2 minutes for this quiz. Have students continue with a different colored pen or pencil when the two minutes are up. After a reasonable time, have students check their work and update their *Multiplication Facts I Know* charts.

A. $2 \times 5 =$ B. $5 \times 7 =$

C. $3 \times 10 =$ D. $10 \times 8 =$

E. $8 \times 5 =$ F. $2 \times 7 =$

G. $5 \times 3 =$ H. $4 \times 5 =$

I. $2 \times 8 =$ J. $10 \times 4 =$

K. $9 \times 2 =$ L. $5 \times 5 =$

M. $5 \times 9 =$ N. $10 \times 5 =$

O. $2 \times 6 =$ P. $6 \times 10 =$

Q. $5 \times 6 =$ R. $4 \times 2 =$

S. $10 \times 7 =$ T. $10 \times 2 =$

U. $5 \times 1 =$ V. $4 \times 2 =$

W. $0 \times 2 =$ X. $10 \times 10 =$

Y. $3 \times 2 =$ Z. $10 \times 9 =$

Three Marbles

A graduated cylinder contains 35 cc of water. Three marbles of the same size are added. The water level rises to 41 cc.

1. Draw two graduated cylinders: one before the marbles are added and one after.

2. What is the volume of each marble?

TIMS Task

1. The first cylinder should be labeled with 35 cc of water. The second cylinder's water level should be higher (41 cc) and have three marbles in it.

2. 2 cc

Lesson ① Measuring Volume

Lesson Overview

Estimated Class Sessions **1**

Working in groups, students estimate the volume of small solid objects, based on models they made from centimeter connecting cubes. Then they measure the actual volume of the objects by determining the amount of water displaced in a graduated cylinder when an object is placed in the cylinder. Students record the estimates and the actual volumes in a data table and analyze the data they collected.

Key Content

- Estimating volume using centimeter connecting cubes.
- Using graduated cylinders to measure volume by displacement.

Key Vocabulary

- cubic centimeter (cc)
- displacement
- graduated cylinder
- liter (l)
- meniscus
- milliliter (ml)
- volume

Homework

1. Assign the Homework section on the *Measuring Volume* Activity Pages.
2. Assign Part 1 of the Home Practice.

Assessment

Use the *Observational Assessment Record* to note students' abilities to measure volume by displacement.

Curriculum Sequence

Before This Unit

Volume

Students measured volume by counting cubes (cubic inches) in Grade 2 Unit 7 *Building with Cubes.* They practiced reading different scales, learned to read a graduated cylinder, and measured volume by displacement in Grade 2 Unit 10 *Exploring Volume.*

After This Unit

3-Dimensional Shapes

Students will explore other properties of 3-dimensional shapes and objects in Unit 18 of Grade 3 *Viewing and Drawing 3-D.*

Volume

Students will further explore the concept of volume in Grade 4 Unit 9 *Shapes and Solids.*

Materials List

Supplies and Copies

Student	Teacher
Supplies for Each Student • centimeter ruler **Supplies for Each Student Group** • small solid objects that fit inside a graduated cylinder (e.g., pens, empty film canisters with lids, lumps of clay, dominoes, glue sticks) • graduated cylinder calibrated no more than 2 cc apart and large enough to hold small objects (250 cc preferred) • eyedropper • beaker or container of water • 2 handfuls of centimeter connecting cubes • several sheets of paper towels	**Supplies**
Copies • 1 copy of *Three-column Data Table* per student (*Unit Resource Guide* Page 34)	**Copies/Transparencies** • 1 transparency of *Scale 1 with Blowup* (*Unit Resource Guide* Page 30) • 1 transparency of *Scale 2 with Blowup* (*Unit Resource Guide* Page 31) • 1 transparency of *Scale 3 with Blowup* (*Unit Resource Guide* Page 32) • 1 transparency of *Meniscus* (*Unit Resource Guide* Page 33) • 1 copy of *Observational Assessment Record* to be used throughout this unit (*Unit Resource Guide* Page 9–10)

All blackline masters including assessment, transparency, and DPP masters are also on the Teacher Resource CD.

Student Books
Measuring Volume (*Student Guide* Pages 236–243)

Daily Practice and Problems and Home Practice
DPP items A–B (*Unit Resource Guide* Pages 12–13)
Home Practice Part 1 (*Discovery Assignment Book* Page 244)

Note: Classrooms whose pacing differs significantly from the suggested pacing of the units should use the Math Facts Calendar in Section 4 of the *Facts Resource Guide* to ensure students receive the complete math facts program.

Assessment Tools
Observational Assessment Record (*Unit Resource Guide* Pages 9–10)

Daily Practice and Problems

Suggestions for using the DPPs are on page 27.

A. Bit: Counting by 0.1s (URG p. 12)

Use your calculator to count by 0.1s starting at any number. Then try these problems.

1. Count by 0.1s to 2. Say the numbers quietly to yourself. Write down the numbers.
2. Count by 0.1s from 9 to 11. Say the numbers quietly to yourself. Write down the numbers.

B. Challenge: Decimal Missing Links (URG p. 13)

Copy each list of numbers below. Find the missing numbers. You may use a calculator.

A. 0.1, 0.2, _____, _____, _____, 0.6
B. 0.7, 0.8, _____, _____, _____, 1.2
C. 9.6, 9.7, 9.8, _____, _____, _____, 10.2
D. 1.5, 2, 2.5, 3, _____, _____, _____, 5
E. 0.3, 0.6, 0.9, _____, _____, _____, 2.1

Make up a problem or two of your own. Trade problems with a friend. Check your friend's work.

Before the Activity

Collect several small objects for students to measure. Students will make models of these objects using centimeter connecting cubes. Avoid objects that allow water to get inside, such as toy cars (unless they are solid), because the volume of their models will not be close to their actual volume measured by displacement. Since wood swells in water, avoid using wooden objects.

Also be careful to select objects that are small enough to fit into (and come out of) the graduated cylinders. Students will have fewer problems fitting objects into large graduated cylinders (250 cc) than small ones (100 cc) although either size can be used. However, very few objects will fit into a 100 cc cylinder, so the activity will not be as rich if you use 100 cc cylinders.

Teaching the Activity

Part 1 Introducing Volume

Students frequently confuse the concepts of mass and volume, since both are ways to describe how large an object is. They studied mass in Unit 9. One way to begin their study of volume is to pose a question whose answer can only make sense if they separate these two concepts.

One such question is on the *Measuring Volume* Activity Pages in the *Student Guide*. "Which is heavier, 1 pound of popcorn or a 1-pound rock?" The answer, of course, is that neither is heavier, they both weigh 1 pound. Suggest other materials to compare in addition to popcorn and rocks. The answer may surprise students because their initial reaction might have been that the rock is heavier. Since both objects have the same weight, ask them to say what variable is different about the objects. Guide them to realize that the objects have a different *volume*.

The *Measuring Volume* Activity Pages define volume for students and describe some common metric units for measuring it—cubic centimeter, milliliter, and liter. Reinforce the students' understanding of a cubic centimeter by asking them to measure the length of each side of a centimeter connecting cube. They will find that each side is 1 centimeter long. Remind students that the volume of a cube with a length of 1 centimeter is **1 cubic centimeter.**

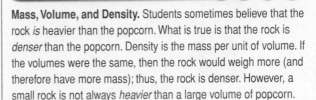

Content Note

Mass, Volume, and Density. Students sometimes believe that the rock *is* heavier than the popcorn. What is true is that the rock is *denser* than the popcorn. Density is the mass per unit of volume. If the volumes were the same, then the rock would weigh more (and therefore have more mass); thus, the rock is denser. However, a small rock is not always *heavier* than a large volume of popcorn.

Measuring Volume

What is volume?

Volume is a measurement of size. It is the amount of space that an object takes up. If the object is a container, like a box or a bottle, then the volume is the amount of space inside it.

A common metric unit of volume is the cubic centimeter. A **cubic centimeter (cc)** is the volume of a cube that is 1 centimeter long on each side.

236   SG • Grade 3 • Unit 16 • Lesson 1   Measuring Volume

Student Guide - page 236

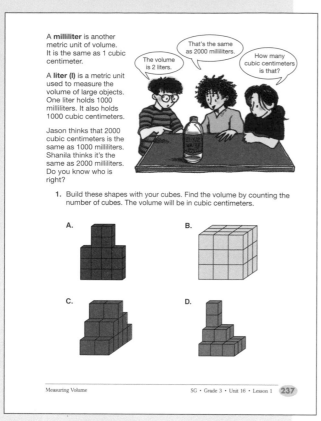

Student Guide - page 237 *(Answers on p. 35)*

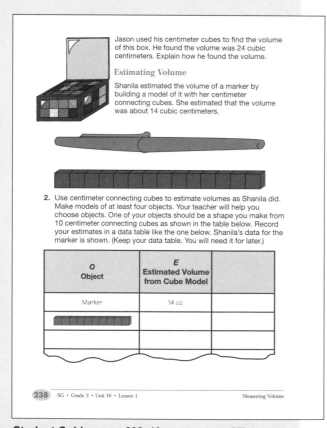

Student Guide - page 238 *(Answers on p. 35)*

Demonstrate building a shape or cube model with centimeter connecting cubes. Display the cube model for students to view. Ask students how they might find the volume of your cube model. Students should suggest counting the number of cubes in the model since each cube has a volume of one cubic centimeter. Find the volume of the cube model by counting the number of cubes. Take it apart if necessary. Encourage students to build cube models and find the volumes. *Question 1* on the *Measuring Volume* Activity Pages provides practice with finding volumes of cube models. Students first build the models, then they count the number of cubes.

Part 2 Estimating Volume

Ask students to brainstorm how they could use centimeter connecting cubes to estimate the volume of one of the small objects you collected. Read the Estimating Volume section on the *Measuring Volume* Activity Pages with students to find out how Shanila estimated the volume of a marker. She used centimeter connecting cubes to make a model about the same size as the marker. She found the volume of the model simply by counting the number of cubes.

Question 2 asks students to estimate the volume of several objects by making models as Shanila did and to record the volume of the models in a table. They should choose at least four objects, including a shape they build from 10 centimeter connecting cubes. There are three columns in the data table. Students should fill in just the first two columns and leave the third blank. This column will be used in Part 4 of this lesson.

Part 3 Measuring the Volume of Liquids

The Measuring the Volume of Liquids section in the *Student Guide* explains how to read the level of a liquid in a graduated cylinder and defines the term **meniscus.**

Content Note

The Meniscus. When we look at a graduated cylinder from the side, we see the meniscus in a cross section. This causes us to see two lines at the top of the water, not one. The upper line is the ring formed as the top of the liquid creeps up the sides of the cylinder. The lower line is the ring formed at the true level of the liquid. Stress that students should read the lower line when reading the level of liquid in a graduated cylinder. The two lines are more pronounced in glass cylinders than in plastic ones.

This activity focuses on the cubic centimeter as the unit used for measuring volume. Some of the graduated cylinders and beakers used by your class may label volume in milliliters. If so, make sure students understand that 1 milliliter is the same volume as 1 cubic centimeter. In this activity students should label their data in cubic centimeters.

Have students practice reading a scale and a meniscus on Transparency Masters of graduated cylinders before they begin their work with actual graduated cylinders. The *Scale 1 with Blowup* Transparency Master can be used for practice in reading scales of 1-cc calibrations with numbers shown every 10 cubic centimeters. The *Scale 2 with Blowup* Transparency Master provides practice reading scales of 2-cc calibrations with numbers shown every 10 cubic centimeters. The *Scale 3 with Blowup* Transparency Master is calibrated in 2-cc increments with numbers shown every 20 cubic centimeters. Have the class practice reading these scales before they work with their graduated cylinders. The *Meniscus* Transparency Master shows students the double-line appearance of a meniscus and points out the correct reading of the lower line for the actual level of the liquid in a cylinder.

Direct students to pour a specific amount of water into their graduated cylinders, for example, 100 cc in a 250-cc graduated cylinder or 50 cc in a 100-cc cylinder. Students should fill the graduated cylinder a little below the desired level and then use an eyedropper to raise the water gradually to the proper level. Stress that the proper way to read a graduated cylinder is to keep it level on the table and to bend down (if necessary) to read it at eye level. If students read it from above or below, the angle their eyes make with the graduated cylinder gives a false reading. This is illustrated for students on the *Measuring Volume* Activity Pages.

Part 4 Measuring the Volume of Solid Objects

The Measuring the Volume of Solid Objects section on the *Measuring Volume* Activity Pages explains how Shanila and Jason found the actual volume of a rock using the displacement method. To measure the volume of a solid object, students fill a graduated

Caution students to put the object in the graduated cylinder very carefully so that no water splashes out. They may accomplish this either by gently dropping the object into the graduated cylinder or by tilting the cylinder and letting the object slide in.

Measuring the Volume of Liquids

When we measure liquids like water and milk, we often use a measuring cup. Scientists use graduated cylinders to measure volume.

To read the level of water in a graduated cylinder, bend down and *put your eyes at the level of the top of the water.* In this picture, only Shanila is reading the water level correctly. Tell why.

It looks like 82 cc from where I stand.

It looks like 80 cc to me!

Water creeps up the sides of a graduated cylinder. It makes a curved surface at the top called a **meniscus.** The meniscus makes it look as though there are two lines on top of each other. You should always *read the lower line.* The lower line shows the level of the water. This cylinder shows a meniscus with a water level of 80 cc. (The meniscus will be more noticeable with glass graduated cylinders than with plastic graduated cylinders.)

Measuring Volume   SG • Grade 3 • Unit 16 • Lesson 1   **239**

Student Guide - page 239

Measuring the Volume of Solid Objects

How can we find the volume of a solid object, such as a rock? A scientist might put the object under water in a graduated cylinder and see how much the water rises.

To find the volume of a rock, Shanila and Jason first put 50 cubic centimeters of water into a graduated cylinder.

Let's start with 50 cc of water. I'll use an eyedropper to put in the last few drops.

Then they slid the rock into the cylinder.

The rock made the water rise from 50 to 63 cubic centimeters.

That means the volume of the rock is 13 cubic centimeters.

How did Jason find the volume of the rock?

240   SG • Grade 3 • Unit 16 • Lesson 1   Measuring Volume

Student Guide - page 240

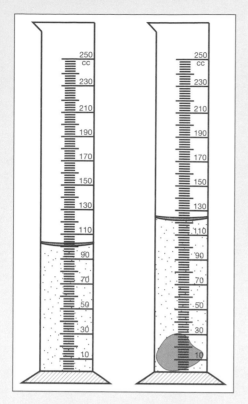

Figure 1: *The rise in the water level after adding a rock*

3. Measure the actual volume of each of the objects you used in Question 2 by holding each object under water in a graduated cylinder. How much higher does the water rise? Record each volume in the last column of your data table.

O Object	E Estimated Volume from Cube Model	V Volume by Displacement
	14 cc	12 cc

Student Guide - page 241 *(Answers on p. 36)*

cylinder with an amount of water that makes it easy for them to calculate the water rise. For instance, if students fill a 250-cc graduated cylinder with 100 cc of water and the water rises to 122 cc when they put the object inside, as in Figure 1, then students can easily subtract 100 from 122 to find the volume, 22 cc.

Explain to students that the object displaces, or pushes aside, its volume in the water, causing the water level to rise. Since the water volume is constant, the new water level can be explained as the volume of the water plus that of the object. To find the volume of the object alone, subtract the starting water level from the final water level.

If the object floats, have students push it under the surface of the water and hold it in place until they can read the level of the water. A thin "pusher," such as the tip of a pencil, a straightened paper clip, or a pin, is better to use than a large pusher because the additional volume of a thin pusher will be minimal. If students use a large pusher, such as a finger, they will not obtain an accurate reading for the object's volume.

Question 3 directs students to find the actual volume of each object from *Question 2,* using the displacement method. As you observe students working, check that they are recording the volume of the objects only and not the volume of the water *and* the objects combined. Figure 2 shows a sample data table with examples of small objects, their estimated volume, and their actual volume.

Journal Prompt

How close were your estimated volumes of the objects to the actual volumes? Discuss why they were not exactly the same. Were some estimates closer than others?

O Object	E Estimated Volume from Cube Model	V Volume by Displacement
shape made from 10 centimeter connecting cubes	10 cc	10 cc
marker	14 cc	12 cc
lump of clay	11 cc	13 cc
domino	6 cc	5 cc

Figure 2: *A sample data table*

Homework and Practice

- The Homework section on the *Measuring Volume* Activity Pages in the *Student Guide* provides practice in reading the scales that appear on graduated cylinders.
- DPP items A and B provide practice with decimals.
- Part 1 of the Home Practice provides practice with multidigit addition and subtraction.

Answers for Part 1 of the Home Practice are in the Answer Key at the end of this lesson and at the end of this unit.

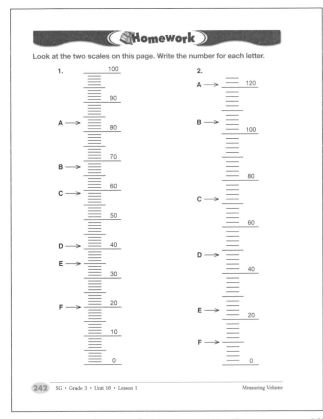

Student Guide - page 242 (Answers on p. 36)

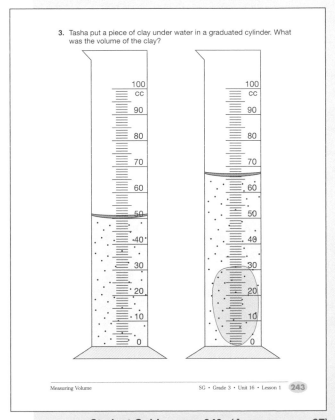

Student Guide - page 243 (Answers on p. 37)

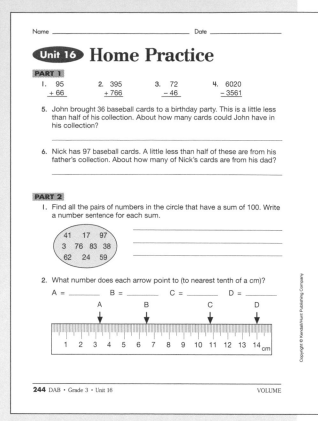

Name _____ **Date** _____

Unit 16 ⬤ Home Practice

PART 1

1. 95
    + 66

2. 395
    + 766

3. 72
    − 46

4. 6020
    − 3561

5. John brought 36 baseball cards to a birthday party. This is a little less than half of his collection. About how many cards could John have in his collection?

_____

6. Nick has 97 baseball cards. A little less than half of these are from his father's collection. About how many of Nick's cards are from his dad?

_____

PART 2

1. Find all the pairs of numbers in the circle that have a sum of 100. Write a number sentence for each sum.

    41 17 97
    3 76 83 38
    62 24 59

    _____
    _____
    _____

2. What number does each arrow point to (to nearest tenth of a cm)?

    A = _____ B = _____ C = _____ D = _____

    A   B   C   D
    1 2 3 4 5 6 7 8 9 10 11 12 13 14 cm

Copyright © Kendall/Hunt Publishing Company

244 DAB • Grade 3 • Unit 16   VOLUME

Discovery Assignment Book - page 244 (Answers on p. 37)

Assessment

Use the *Observational Assessment Record* to document students' abilities to measure volume by displacement.

Extension

Challenge students to find a way to measure the volume of an object that is too big to fit inside a graduated cylinder. One method is to put a container large enough to hold the object inside a pan. Fill the container to the brim with water and place the object inside the container. The object will displace an amount of water equal to its volume. Pour the over-flow of water from the pan into a graduated cylinder to measure the object's volume. Another way is to use a graduated cylinder to calibrate a large jar to be used as a graduated cylinder. See the TIMS Tutor: *The Concept of Volume* for further discussion as well as instructions on how to do this.

Estimated Class Sessions

1

At a Glance

Math Facts and Daily Practice and Problems
DPP items A and B provide practice with decimals.

Part 1. Introducing Volume
1. Discuss the concepts of mass and volume using the *Measuring Volume* Activity Pages in the *Student Guide.*
2. Students measure the length, width, and height of a centimeter connecting cube and find that its volume is a cubic centimeter.
3. Students build cube models and find their volume by counting the number of cubes.
4. Students complete *Question 1* on the *Measuring Volume* Activity Pages.

Part 2. Estimating Volume
1. Students use centimeter connecting cubes to estimate the volume of objects.
2. Students fill in two columns of a data table to complete *Question 2.*

Part 3. Measuring the Volume of Liquids
1. Students practice reading a scale and a meniscus with the help of transparency masters.
2. Students fill graduated cylinders to a desired level with the help of an eyedropper.

Part 4. Measuring the Volume of Solid Objects
1. Students use graduated cylinders to measure the volumes of the objects they chose in *Question 2.*
2. To answer *Question 3,* students fill in the third column of the data table begun in *Question 2.*

Homework
1. Assign the Homework section on the *Measuring Volume* Activity Pages.
2. Assign Part 1 of the Home Practice.

Assessment
Use the *Observational Assessment Record* to note students' abilities to measure volume by displacement.

Extension
Challenge students to find a way to measure the volume of an object that is too big to fit in the graduated cylinder.

Answer Key is on pages 35–37.

Notes:

Scale 1 with Blowup

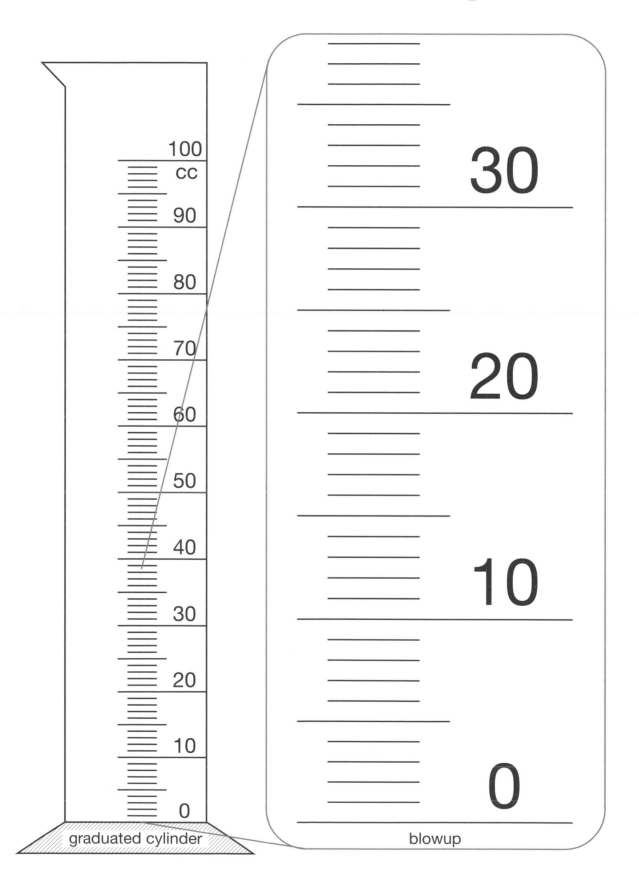

graduated cylinder

blowup

Copyright © Kendall/Hunt Publishing Company

Transparency Master

Scale 2 with Blowup

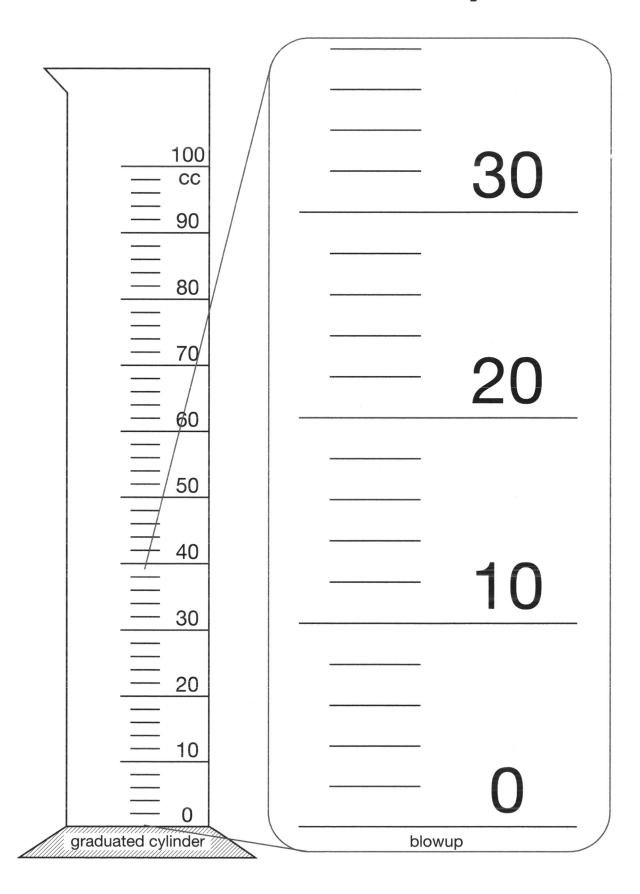

graduated cylinder

blowup

Copyright © Kendall/Hunt Publishing Company

Scale 3 with Blowup

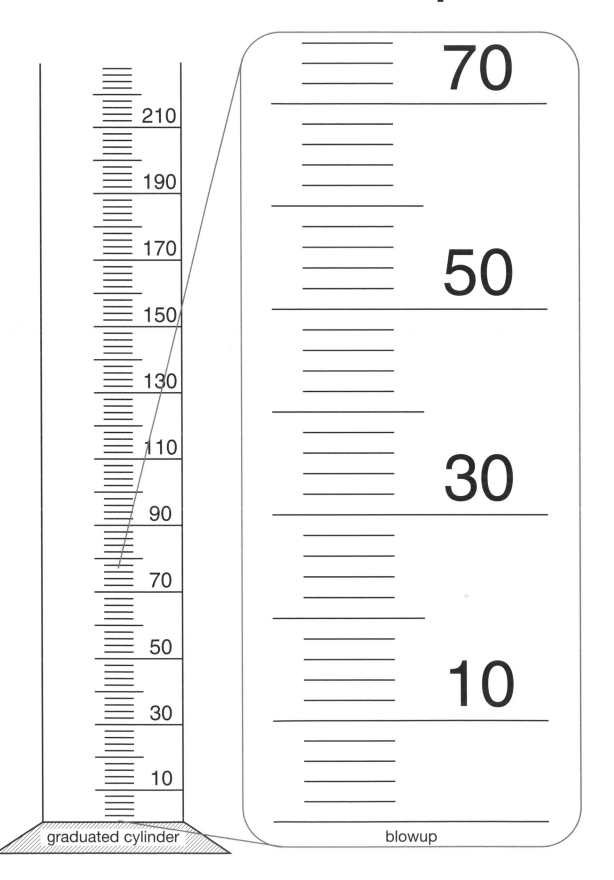

graduated cylinder

blowup

Copyright © Kendall/Hunt Publishing Company

Transparency Master

Meniscus

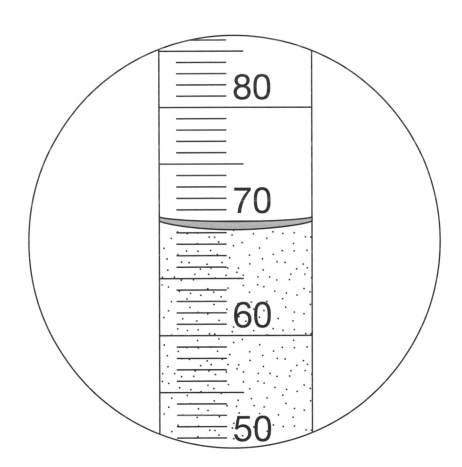

Copyright © Kendall/Hunt Publishing Company

Name _____ Date _____

_____

Copyright © Kendall/Hunt Publishing Company

Three-column Data Table, Blackline Master

Student Guide (pp. 237–238)

1. **A.** 16 cc

   B. 27 cc

   C. 18 cc

   D. 15 cc

2. See Figure 2 in the Lesson Guide for a sample data table for *Question 2.**

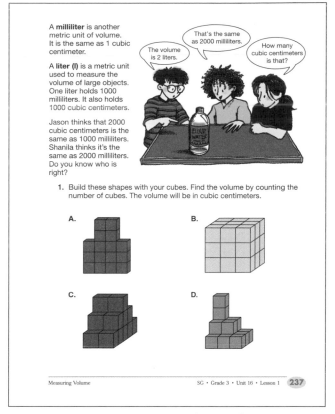

Student Guide - page 237

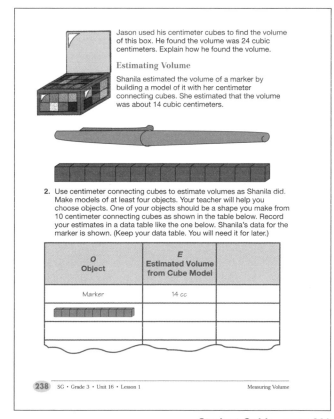

Student Guide - page 238

*Answers and/or discussion are included in the Lesson Guide.

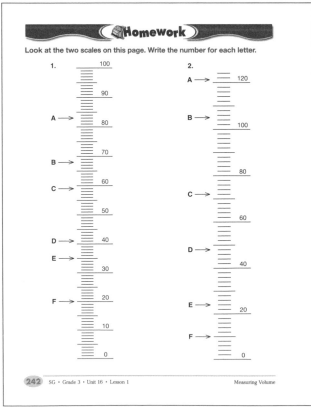

Student Guide - page 241

Student Guide - page 242

Student Guide (p. 241)

3. See Figure 2 in the Lesson Guide for a sample data table for *Question 3.**

Student Guide (p. 242)

Homework

1. **A.** 83 cc
   B. 68 cc
   C. 59 cc
   D. 41 cc
   E. 35 cc
   F. 20 cc
2. **A.** 121 cc
   B. 105 cc
   C. 72 cc
   D. 48 cc
   E. 24 cc
   F. 10 cc

*Answers and/or discussion are included in the Lesson Guide.

Student Guide (p. 243)

3. 16 cc

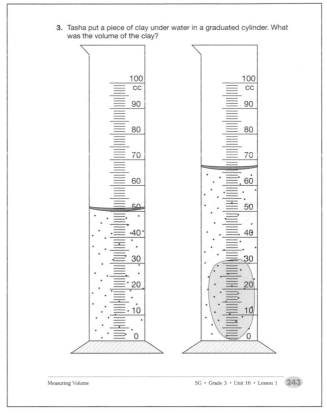

Student Guide - page 243

Discovery Assignment Book (p. 244)

Home Practice*

Part 1

1. 161
2. 1161
3. 26
4. 2459
5. about 73–80 cards
6. about 45–48 cards

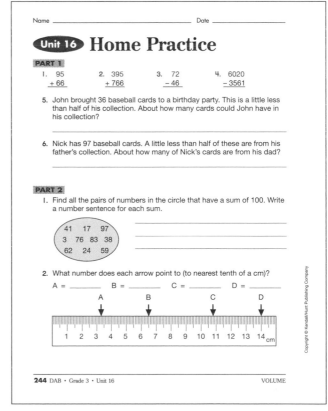

Discovery Assignment Book - page 244

*Answers for all the Home Practice in the *Discovery Assignment Book* are at the end of the unit.

Lesson 2

Fill 'er Up!

Estimated Class Sessions

3

Lesson Overview

In this lab, students develop a plan for accurately finding the volume of large containers. They find the volumes of at least three containers of various sizes and shapes. Students use addition, subtraction, multiplication, and division to solve problems involving volume. In working with containers of different shapes, the students are reminded that the tallest container may not always have the largest volume.

Key Content

- Collecting, organizing, graphing, and analyzing data.
- Measuring accurately the volume of large, unusually shaped containers.
- Measuring volume using graduated cylinders.
- Solving addition, subtraction, multiplication, and division problems involving volume.

- Adding, subtracting, multiplying, and dividing multidigit numbers.
- Making and interpreting a bar graph.
- Using patterns in data to make predictions and solve problems.
- Dealing with precision and accuracy,
- Using medians to average data.

Math Facts

DPP Bits C, E, and G provide practice with multiplication facts for the 2s, 5s, and 10s.

Homework

1. For homework students finish questions not completed in class.
2. Assign Parts 2 and 3 of the Home Practice.
3. Students continue to practice the multiplication facts for the 2s, 5s, and 10s using their *Triangle Flash Cards*.
4. Assign *Questions 1–2* on the *Volume Hunt* Activity Pages for Lesson 3 in the *Discovery Assignment Book*.

Assessment

1. Use *Questions 10–11* on the *Fill 'er Up!* Lab Pages to assess students' understanding of how to measure volume.
2. Assign scores to one or more parts of the lab.
3. Use the *Observational Assessment Record* to note students' abilities to collect, organize, graph, and analyze data.
4. Use DPP Task F Volume as a quiz.

Medians

Students used medians to average data from three trials in experiments in Grade 3 Unit 5 Lessons 2 and 3 and Unit 15 Lesson 2 *Measuring to the Nearest Tenth*.

Developing Number Concepts and Procedures Using Data

Students used multiplication to solve problems involving area in Grade 3 Unit 5 Lesson 3 *The Better "Picker Upper,"* multiplication and division to investigate perimeter of regular shapes in Unit 7 Lesson 6 *Walking around Shapes,* addition and multiplication to solve problems involving mass in Unit 9 Lesson 2 *Mass vs. Number,* and multiplication to solve problems involving length in Unit 10 Lesson 1 *Stencilrama.* They developed decimal concepts while measuring to the nearest tenth of a centimeter in Unit 15 Lesson 4 *Length vs. Number.*

Materials List

Supplies and Copies

Student	Teacher
Supplies for Each Student Group • 1 small, 1 medium, and 1 large container • 250 cc graduated cylinder • eyedropper • paper towels • cup or small container • container such as a dishpan	**Supplies** • large irregularly-shaped "mystery" jar
Copies • 1 copy of *Centimeter Graph Paper* per student (*Unit Resource Guide* Page 51) • 1 copy of *Three-trial Data Table* per student, optional (*Unit Resource Guide* Page 52) • 1 copy of *Triangle Flash Cards 2s, 5s,* and *10s* per student, optional (*Unit Resource Guide* Pages 53–55)	**Copies/Transparencies**

All blackline masters including assessment, transparency, and DPP masters are also on the Teacher Resource CD.

Student Books
Fill 'er Up! (*Student Guide* Pages 244–248)
Volume Hunt (*Discovery Assignment Book* Page 247)

Daily Practice and Problems and Home Practice
DPP items C–H (*Unit Resource Guide* Pages 13–16)
Home Practice Parts 2–3 (*Discovery Assignment Book* Pages 244–245)

Note: Classrooms whose pacing differs significantly from the suggested pacing of the units should use the Math Facts Calendar in Section 4 of the *Facts Resource Guide* to ensure students receive the complete math facts program.

Assessment Tools
Observational Assessment Record (*Unit Resource Guide* Pages 9–10)

Daily Practice and Problems

Suggestions for using the DPPs are on pages 47–48.

C. Bit: Doubles (URG p. 13)

A. $2 \times 6 =$ B. $12 + 12 =$
C. $4 \times 6 =$ D. $2 \times 5 =$
E. $10 + 10 =$ F. $4 \times 5 =$
G. $2 \times 10 =$ H. $20 + 20 =$
I. $4 \times 10 =$

What patterns do you see? Describe a strategy for multiplying a number by 4.

F. Task: Volume (URG p. 15)

This is 1 cubic centimeter:

1. What is the volume of each of the following shapes?

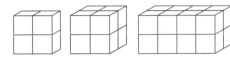

2. For each of the shapes above, use connecting cubes to build a different shape with the same volume.

D. Task: Walk-a-thon (URG p. 14)

The following are the results of a walk-a-thon.

Second Grade   Third Grade
Room 100 $214   Room 200 $147
Room 101 $161   Room 201 $262

1. How much did the Second Grade raise?
2. How much did the Third Grade raise?
3. Which grade came closer to the goal of $450?
4. How much more did Room 201 raise than Room 200?

G. Bit: More Doubles (URG p. 15)

A. $3 \times 7 =$ B. $21 + 21 =$
C. $6 \times 7 =$ D. $3 \times 8 =$
E. $24 + 24 =$ F. $6 \times 8 =$
G. $3 \times 10 =$ H. $30 + 30 =$
I. $6 \times 10 =$

What patterns do you see? Describe a strategy for multiplying a number by 6.

E. Bit: Multiplication Patterns
(URG p. 14)

A. $1 \times 5 =$ $2 \times 5 =$ $3 \times 5 =$
   $4 \times 5 =$ $5 \times 5 =$ $6 \times 5 =$
   $7 \times 5 =$ $8 \times 5 =$ $9 \times 5 =$
   $10 \times 5 =$
B. $1 \times 10 =$ $2 \times 10 =$ $3 \times 10 =$
   $4 \times 10 =$ $5 \times 10 =$ $6 \times 10 =$
   $7 \times 10 =$ $8 \times 10 =$ $9 \times 10 =$
   $10 \times 10 =$

What patterns do you see in both sets of problems?

H. Task: Messy Student (URG p. 16)

A messy student spilled some ink on a math paper. These problems have ink on them. Can you figure out what is covered up?

1. $\begin{array}{r} \overset{1}{5}6 \\ + \\ \hline 91 \end{array}$ 2. $\begin{array}{r} \overset{1}{}3 \\ + 2 \\ \hline 80 \end{array}$ 3. $\begin{array}{r} 3 \\ + \\ \hline 72 \end{array}$

Collect containers of various sizes and shapes so each group of students will have at least three containers. Jars work quite well for this investigation because they come in a variety of sizes and shapes. Cups, such as small 3-oz paper cups, medium 9-oz coffee cups, and large 16-oz plastic cups, can also be used. However, using only cups is not as much fun since they all have the same shape.

The labels on some jars give their volumes, but usually in fluid ounces, not cubic centimeters. Note that 1 fluid ounce equals about 30 cubic centimeters.

The labels on other jars give the weight of the contents, but not the volume. If possible, remove all labels before giving the jars to the students. The following list provides ranges of volumes for some common jars.

SUGGESTIONS FOR JAR COLLECTING

Small Jars V = 150 to 250 cc (5 to 8 oz)	Medium Jars V = 500 to 700 cc (16 to 23 oz)	Large Jars V = 950 to 1000 cc (about 32 oz)
baby food small jelly small olive tomato paste	peanut butter applesauce salsa	mayonnaise 1-quart juice container 1-liter bottled water

Figure 3: *Volumes of some common jars*

Set aside a "mystery jar," whose volume children will guess after they have completed the lab.

Teaching the Lab

Part 1 Launching the Investigation

The first page of the *Fill 'er Up!* Lab Pages in the *Student Guide* asks students to help Andrea make a plan to find out which of her containers has the larger volume. This activity launches the lab by allowing small groups of children to try out their equipment with water and to investigate different ways to find volume before they begin the lab. If all groups are given the same size container, they can compare with each other to see how accurate they are. A good container for this is a large paper cup, about 2 to 3 times the size of their graduated cylinders.

TIMS Tip

When estimating volume, children often look only at the height of a container instead of considering all its dimensions. For this reason, you may want to choose containers so that the tallest is not always the one with the largest volume.

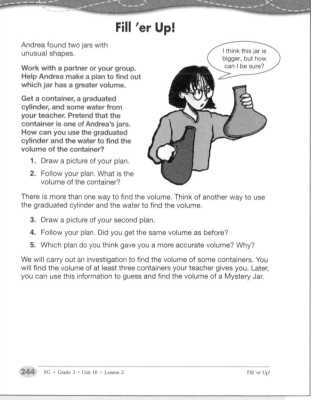

Fill 'er Up!

Andrea found two jars with unusual shapes.

I think this jar is bigger, but how can I be sure?

Work with a partner or your group. Help Andrea make a plan to find out which jar has a greater volume.

Get a container, a graduated cylinder, and some water from your teacher. Pretend that the container is one of Andrea's jars. How can you use the graduated cylinder and the water to find the volume of the container?

1. Draw a picture of your plan.
2. Follow your plan. What is the volume of the container?

There is more than one way to find the volume. Think of another way to use the graduated cylinder and the water to find the volume.

3. Draw a picture of your second plan.
4. Follow your plan. Did you get the same volume as before?
5. Which plan do you think gave you a more accurate volume? Why?

We will carry out an investigation to find the volume of some containers. You will find the volume of at least three containers your teacher gives you. Later, you can use this information to guess and find the volume of a Mystery Jar.

244   SG • Grade 3 • Unit 16 • Lesson 2   Fill 'er Up!

Student Guide - page 244 *(Answers on p. 56)*

Ask groups to present their plans to the class. They will probably come up with at least one of two basic ways to measure volume:

1. One way is to pour the water from the jar into the graduated cylinder and to count the number of times the graduated cylinder is filled. Any water left after the last complete fill can be poured into the graduated cylinder and easily measured.

2. The second way is to pour water from the graduated cylinder into the jar and to count the number of times it takes to fill the jar. The amount left in the cylinder after the jar is filled is then subtracted from the full amount to determine how much was poured out the last time. For example, suppose 250 cc are poured from the graduated cylinder into the jar twice. Then, the third pour fills the jar to the top with 70 cc remaining in the graduated cylinder. The volume of the container is 250 cc + 250 cc + (250 cc − 70 cc) = 680 cc.

Encourage students to try both ways and to discuss the pros and cons of each way. The second method described is usually more accurate than the first method. Although the first method is a very natural way to measure the volume, it is likely to involve a lot of spilling, unless students are using containers such as bottles with narrow spouts, where spilling would be minimal. Both methods use an eyedropper to set the level in the graduated cylinder at exactly 250 cc (or 100 cc if they are using the smaller graduated cylinders). Remind students to be as accurate as possible.

Part 2 Identifying Variables and Drawing the Picture

After students have explored different ways to find a container's volume and can do it reasonably accurately, they are ready to begin the lab. The *Fill 'er Up!* Lab Pages help children organize their investigation according to the TIMS Laboratory Method: drawing a picture, collecting and organizing data in a data table, graphing the data, and analyzing the data.

Start the lab by giving each group at least three containers of different sizes. Ask students to identify the two main variables of the investigation. One variable is Container. They select its values (e.g., red cup, peanut butter jar, tall jar) before they begin. The other variable is Volume. They will find its values during the experiment.

TIMS Tip

You may want groups to work with their containers, graduated cylinders, water, and cups inside a dishpan that would collect any spills.

TIMS Tip

Because of the surface tension of water, it is possible to fill a container a little higher than the top. Direct students to fill their jars only to the top so they don't measure more than the container's actual volume.

Once the variables are identified, students draw a picture of the investigation. Remind students that the purpose of their drawing is to communicate the details of how they will conduct their experiment. They should indicate their method of finding the volume: Are they pouring water from the cylinder to the container or from the container to the cylinder? Their pictures should show the relative sizes and shapes of their containers along with the names that the containers will be given in the data table (e.g., red cup, peanut butter jar, tall jar). Figure 4 shows a sample picture.

Figure 4: *A sample picture*

Part 3 **Collecting and Recording the Data**
Students are now ready to collect data and record it in a data table. At this point in the *Math Trailblazers* curriculum, most of your students can draw on lined paper a data table similar to the one on the *Fill 'er Up!* Lab Pages. Or, provide copies of the *Three-trial Data Table* and have children fill in the headings. Remind students to include units in their tables.

Fill 'er Up

Container	Volume in ___cc___ unit			
	Trial 1	Trial 2	Trial 3	Median
jelly jar	230 cc	228 cc	233 cc	230 cc
mayonnaise jar	902 cc	910 cc	914 cc	910 cc
corn oil jar	1560 cc	1541 cc	1550 cc	1550 cc

Figure 5: *A completed data table*

Explain to students that they will measure the volume of each container three times and record the results under "Trial 1," "Trial 2," and "Trial 3" in the data table. By measuring each volume three times, students should obtain more accurate data. Then, they can graph the median of the three readings.

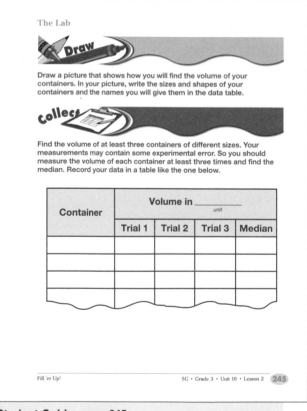

Student Guide - page 245

Students sometimes feel that they *must* record all data they take. However, one reason they conduct more than one trial is to detect errors in their data. If one of their three trials shows a value very different from the others, then it should be repeated. If repeating the trial confirms that the original value is probably incorrect, then it should be deleted and the new value recorded. Assure your students that this is not "cheating." Judging the reasonableness of results is part of proper scientific procedure.

Discuss with students the reason a bar graph is appropriate, but a point graph is not. We use a point graph when it makes sense to ask about values between data points. For example, in *Mass vs. Number* in Unit 9, *Using Patterns to Predict,* students measured the mass of 4 and 6 trapezoids and could ask about the mass of 5 or even $4\frac{1}{2}$ trapezoids. The point graph enabled us to interpolate those inbetween masses. When graphing the volume of different containers, it doesn't make sense to ask about the volumes of containers "between the red and the blue container" or "between container A and container B." Therefore, a line connecting the data points on a graph of the containers' volumes would not have meaning.

Figure 6 is a sample graph of our data. Note that the axes are labeled with the variable names and units and that the lines are numbered, not the spaces. The sample graph shows the vertical axis numbered by 100s. Students may number the vertical axis differently, depending on the size of the numbers they obtain.

Part 4 Exploring the Data
In *Questions 6–8,* students explore their data and use it to make predictions. Remind students to use the median values in their data tables or graphs to answer these questions.

The steps outlined in *Question 8* provide an excellent opportunity to use the collected data to investigate division concepts. Students must predict the number of full small containers that can be poured into the largest container. Then they must find the amount of water needed to fill the large container the rest of the way. This scenario is a classic division problem. However, students may use addition, subtraction, or multiplication as well.

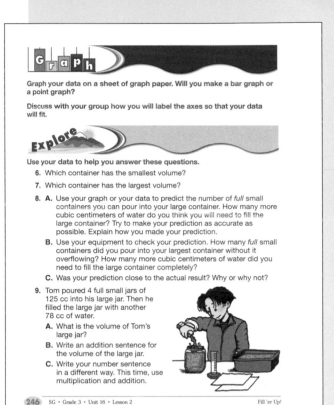

Graph your data on a sheet of graph paper. Will you make a bar graph or a point graph?

Discuss with your group how you will label the axes so that your data will fit.

Use your data to help you answer these questions.

6. Which container has the smallest volume?

7. Which container has the largest volume?

8. **A.** Use your graph or your data to predict the number of *full* small containers you can pour into your large container. How many more cubic centimeters of water do you think you will need to fill the large container? Try to make your prediction as accurate as possible. Explain how you made your prediction.

   B. Use your equipment to check your prediction. How many *full* small containers did you pour into your largest container without it overflowing? How many more cubic centimeters of water did you need to fill the large container completely?

   C. Was your prediction close to the actual result? Why or why not?

9. Tom poured 4 full small jars of 125 cc into his large jar. Then he filled the large jar with another 78 cc of water.

   A. What is the volume of Tom's large jar?

   B. Write an addition sentence for the volume of the large jar.

   C. Write your number sentence in a different way. This time, use multiplication and addition.

246   SG • Grade 3 • Unit 16 • Lesson 2   Fill 'er Up!

Student Guide - page 246 (Answers on p. 56)

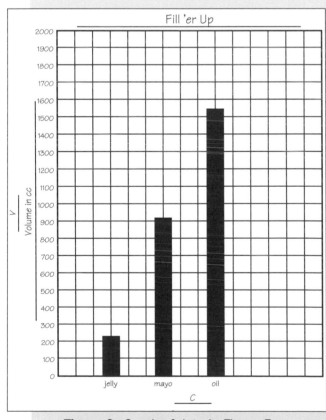

Figure 6: *Graph of data in Figure 5*

TIMS Tip

Multiples on the Calendar is a daily activity that was introduced in Unit 3 *Exploring Multiplication*. If your class has been doing that activity, you may want to make a connection between the number sentences they have been writing daily, such as $4 \times 5 + 3 = 23$, and the number sentence they are to write for **Question 4C**, such as 4×125 cc $+ 78$ cc $= 578$ cc.

---

10. Molly fills her 80 cc graduated cylinder with water and empties it into a jar four times. The jar is still not full. She fills the graduated cylinder again. She uses this water to fill the jar to the top. Her graduated cylinder still has 25 cc of water in it. What is the volume of the jar? Show your work.

11. Mimi has a small jar with a volume of 40 cc and a bigger jar with a volume of 230 cc.
    A. How many *full* small jars of water can Mimi pour into her big jar? How much more water does she need to fill the big jar to the top? Show your work.
    B. Write a number sentence for your answer.

12. A container has a volume of 240 cc. You have many small jars, each with a volume of 45 cc. You want to pour all the water from the big container into the small jars.
    A. About how many jars can you fill? First, write down your estimate. Then solve the problem.
    B. How much water will be in the last jar?
    C. Write a division sentence for the problem.

Fill 'er Up!   SG • Grade 3 • Unit 16 • Lesson 2   **247**

Student Guide - page 247 *(Answers on p. 57)*

After they fill the small container for the last time and pour as much as they can into the large container, they will need to figure out how much water they just poured. To do this, students can use a graduated cylinder to measure the amount left in the small jar and then subtract that number from the amount the small container holds.

Question 8C asks whether their prediction was close to their actual result. This should generate a discussion of what it means to be "close." Scientists often measure closeness in terms of percent error. For now, you can have the class vote on what they feel "close" should be. They might agree that "within 1 cc" is probably too much to expect but that "within 5 or 10 cc" is a reasonable standard for closeness. Sometimes children go back to their predictions and change them to match their results. Explain that although their predictions should be "close," they are not expected to be exact. In fact, it would be very unusual for their predictions to match their experimental results exactly.

Question 9 uses fictitious data to prompt students to write additional number sentences. ***Questions 10–13*** are aimed at checking children's understanding of the work they have done by asking them to relate it to similar situations.

Question 12 asks what happens when we empty a 240-cc container into several 45 cc jars. This provides another opportunity to explore division with a remainder. ***Question 12A*** has students estimate the number of small jars they can fill. They can do this by rounding 45 cc up to 50 cc. Since 5×50 cc $= 250$ cc, a reasonable estimate is 5 jars.

Let children solve the problem in whatever way is natural to them. They may choose to solve it by subtracting 45 cc repeatedly, beginning with 240 cc and ending when an amount less than 45 cc is left. They will find that they subtract 5 times and have 15 cc remaining. Another way is to add 45 cc to itself until they almost reach 240 cc and then calculate how much is left over. Using a calculator, they would get 240 cc $\div 45$ cc $= 5.3333333$.

Although children are not ready yet to discuss the exact meaning of this decimal representation of the remainder, you can explain that the calculator answer means that they can fill five small jars and have some water left over. To calculate the amount left over, they first would multiply 5×45 cc and get 225 cc. Then, they would subtract 225 cc from 240 cc and get 15 cc.

Question 13 evaluates the students' understanding that the tallest jar does not always have the greatest volume. Jar B is the tallest, and jar C is the widest. Since it takes more jar As to fill jar C than it does to fill jar B, jar C has the greater volume. Some children may trust their eyes more than their heads and select jar B in spite of the data.

Journal Prompt

How would you use a graduated cylinder to find the volume of a jar that is larger than the cylinder? Describe your answer in your own words.

Math Facts

DPP items C, E, and G provide practice with the multiplication facts for the 2s, 5s, and 10s.

Homework and Practice

- **Questions 10–13** on the *Fill 'er Up!* Lab Pages in the *Student Guide* may be assigned as homework.
- DPP Tasks D and H provide multidigit addition and subtraction practice.
- Remind students to continue to practice the multiplication facts for the 2s, 5s, and 10s, using their *Triangle Flash Cards.* Let students know when you will give the Multiplication Quiz: 2s, 5s, and 10s.
- In Lesson 3 *Volume Hunt,* the first part of the activity is done at home. When your class completes the lab in this lesson, assign as homework **Questions 1–2** from the *Volume Hunt* Activity Pages in the *Discovery Assignment Book.* Students will then be prepared for the in-class activity in Lesson 3.
- Assign Parts 2 and 3 of the Home Practice for homework. Part 2 builds number sense. Part 3 is a set of word problems.

Answers for Parts 2 and 3 of the Home Practice are in the Answer Key at the end of this lesson and at the end of this unit.

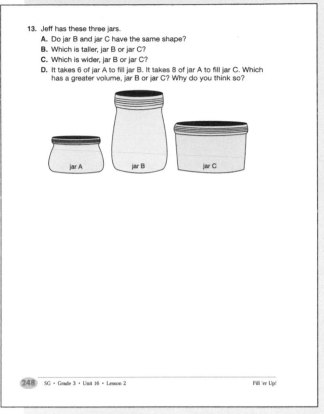

Student Guide - page 248 *(Answers on p. 57)*

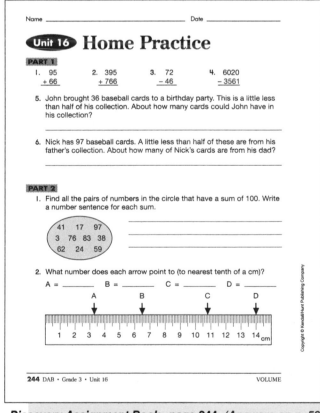

Discovery Assignment Book - page 244 *(Answers on p. 58)*

Name _____ Date _____

PART 3

1. You are given a balance and some 8-gram, 5-gram, and 1-gram masses. How many of each would you need to balance an object with a mass of 78 grams? Show your work.

_____

_____

2. A graduated cylinder is filled with 40 cc of water. Four marbles of the same size are added to the cylinder. The level of the water rises to 52 cc. What is the volume of each marble? Show your work.

_____

_____

3. Tanya's parents told her that if she can save $100.00 towards a new bike, they will pay the rest. So far she has saved $20.00. She makes $9.00 every Saturday baby-sitting. How many weeks will it take Tanya to save $100.00? Show your work.

_____

_____

PART 4

1. How many hops will a +2 mathhopper take to reach or go past 100 if it starts on 0? Show your work on a piece of paper. _____

2. How many hops will a +5 mathhopper need to take to reach 1000 if it starts at 0? Show your work on a piece of paper. _____

3. If a +10 mathhopper starts at 5 and takes 8 hops, on what number will it land? Show your work on a piece of paper. _____

VOLUME   DAB • Grade 3 • Unit 16 **245**

Discovery Assignment Book - page 245 (Answers on p. 58)

Name _____ Date _____

Volume Hunt

At Home

1. Find two containers of different sizes: 1 cup, 1 pint, 1 quart, or 1 gallon. Fill the smaller container with water, and empty it into the larger container. How many times can you do this without making the larger container overflow?

2. If your smaller container is a cup, answer Question 2A.
   If your smaller container is a pint, answer Question 2B.
   If your smaller container is a quart, answer Question 2C.

   A. How many cups are in a _____?
      size of larger container
      _____ cups

   B. How many pints are in a _____?
      size of larger container
      _____ pints

   C. How many quarts are in a _____?
      size of larger container
      _____ quarts

Volume Hunt   DAB • Grade 3 • Unit 16 • Lesson 3 **247**

Discovery Assignment Book - page 247 (Answers on p. 59)

Assessment

- *Questions 10–11* on the *Fill 'er Up!* Lab Pages can be used to assess students' understanding of how to find the volume of a container.

- Assign scores to one or more parts of the lab. For example, grade students' graphs. Look for a title, correct labels on the axes, appropriate scales, and bars drawn correctly. See Evaluating Labs in the Assessment section of the *Teacher Implementation Guide* for more information.

- Use the *Observational Assessment Record* to note students' abilities to collect, organize, graph, and analyze data.

- Use DPP Task F to assess students' abilities to find volume by counting cubic centimeters.

Extension

Challenge children to estimate and find the volume of a "mystery jar," whose shape is irregular.

Math Facts and Daily Practice and Problems

DPP Bits C, E, and G provide practice with multiplication facts for the 2s, 5s, and 10s. Tasks D and H provide computation practice. Task F reviews finding volume.

Part 1. Launching the Investigation

1. Students read the first page of the *Fill 'er Up!* Lab Pages in the *Student Guide*.
2. Students develop and share methods for measuring the volume of an irregular container.
3. Groups try out at least two different ways to find the volumes of containers using their equipment and water.
4. Students discuss the pros and cons of each method.

Part 2. Identifying Variables and Drawing the Picture

1. Give each group at least three containers of different sizes.
2. Ask students to identify the two main variables of the investigation: Container and Volume.
3. Students draw a picture of the investigation.

Part 3. Collecting and Recording the Data

1. Students prepare a data table. They may draw their own table similar to the one on the *Fill 'er Up!* Lab Pages or they may use a *Three-trial Data Table.*
2. Students measure the volume of each container three times and record the results under "Trial 1," "Trial 2," and "Trial 3" in the data table. They find the median value of the three trials.
3. Discuss with students the reason a bar graph is appropriate and a point graph is not.
4. Students graph the median values of their data using *Centimeter Graph Paper*.

Part 4. Exploring the Data

1. In **Questions 6–8** students explore their own data and use it to make predictions.
2. Students complete **Questions 9–13** in class if time allows or at home.
3. Students estimate the volume of a "mystery" jar.

At a Glance

Homework

1. For homework students finish questions not completed in class.
2. Assign Parts 2 and 3 of the Home Practice.
3. Students continue to practice the multiplication facts for the 2s, 5s, and 10s using their *Triangle Flash Cards.*
4. Assign *Questions 1–2* on the *Volume Hunt* Activity Pages for Lesson 3 in the *Discovery Assignment Book.*

Assessment

1. Use *Questions 10–11* on the *Fill 'er Up!* Lab Pages to assess students' understanding of how to measure volume.
2. Assign scores to one or more parts of the lab.
3. Use the *Observational Assessment Record* to note students' abilities to collect, organize, graph, and analyze data.
4. Use DPP Task F Volume as a quiz.

Extension

Challenge students to estimate and find the volume of a "mystery jar" whose shape is irregular.

Answer Key is on pages 56–59.

Notes:

Name _____ Date _____

Copyright © Kendall/Hunt Publishing Company

Centimeter Graph Paper, Blackline Master

Name _____ Date _____

_____

	Trial 1	Trial 2	Trial 3	Average

Copyright © Kendall/Hunt Publishing Company

Three-trial Data Table, Blackline Master

Triangle Flash Cards: 2s

- Work with a partner. Each partner cuts out the flash cards below.

- Your partner chooses one card at a time and covers the shaded corner.

- Multiply the two uncovered numbers.

- Divide the used cards into three piles: those you know and can answer quickly, those you can figure out, and those you need to learn.

- Practice the last two piles again. Then make a list of the facts you need to practice at home.

- Repeat the directions for your partner.

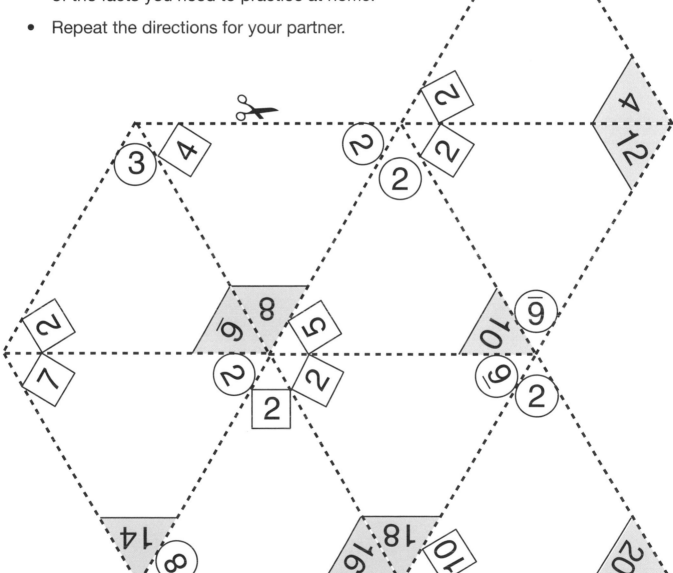

Copyright © Kendall/Hunt Publishing Company

Triangle Flash Cards: 5s

- Work with a partner. Each partner cuts out the flash cards below.

- Your partner chooses one card at a time and covers the shaded corner.

- Multiply the two uncovered numbers.

- Divide the used cards into three piles: those you know and can answer quickly, those you can figure out, and those you need to learn.

- Practice the last two piles again. Then make a list of the facts you need to practice at home.

- Repeat the directions for your partner.

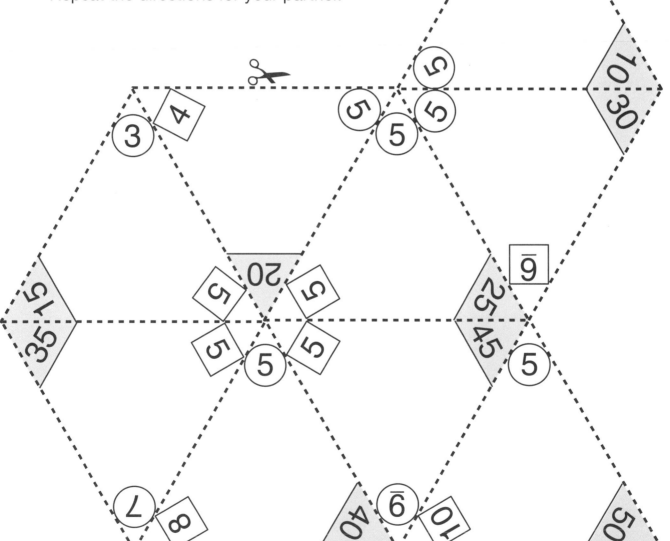

Copyright © Kendall/Hunt Publishing Company

Triangle Flash Cards: 10s

- Work with a partner. Each partner cuts out the 9 flash cards below.

- Your partner chooses one card at a time and covers the shaded corner.

- Multiply the two uncovered numbers.

- Divide the used cards into three piles: those you know and can answer quickly, those you can figure out, and those you need to learn.

- Practice the last two piles again. Then make a list of the facts you need to practice at home.

- Repeat the directions for your partner.

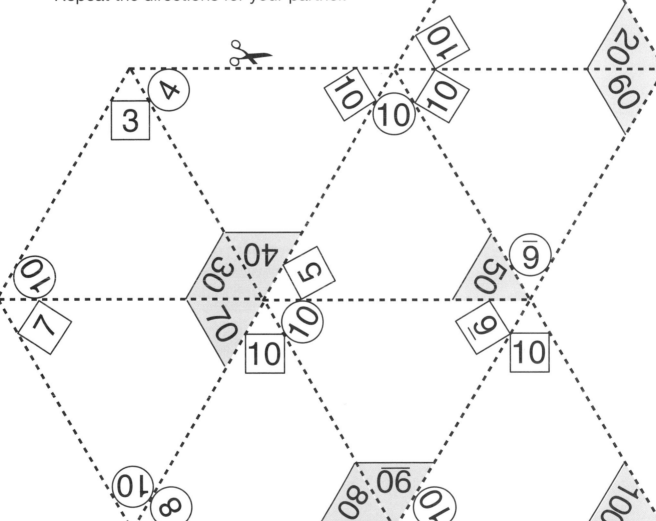

Copyright © Kendall/Hunt Publishing Company

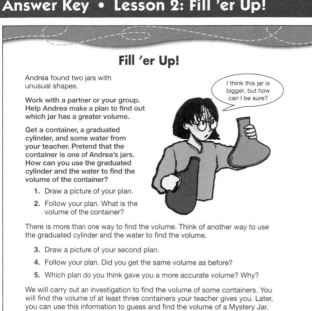

Student Guide - page 244

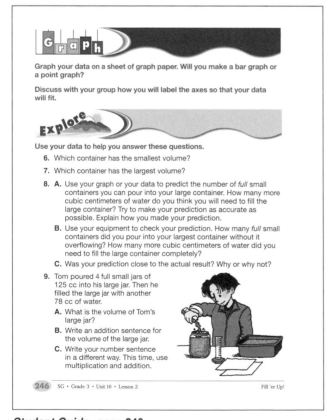

Student Guide - page 246

*Answers and/or discussion are included in the Lesson Guide.

Student Guide (p. 244)

Fill 'er Up!*

See Part 1 of Teaching the Lab in Lesson Guide 2 for two possible strategies students may use to find the volume of a container.

Student Guide (p. 246)

See Figures 4, 5, and 6 in the Lesson Guide for a sample picture, data table, and graph. The answers to *Questions 6–8* below are based on the data in these figures.

6. jelly jar

7. corn oil jar

8. **A.** 6 jelly jars would give 1380 cc. We need 170 cc more to fill the large container.

   B. Answers will vary.

   C. Answers will vary.

9. **A.** 578 cc

   B. $125 + 125 + 125 + 125 + 78 = 578$ cc

   C. $125 \times 4 + 78 = 578$ cc

Student Guide (p. 247)

10. $80 + 80 + 80 + 80 + 55 = 375$ cc

11. A. 5 small jars will give 200 cc; 30 cc more will be needed.

B. Sentences will vary. Possible sentence: $40 \times 5 + 30 = 230$ cc

12. A. Estimates will vary. You can fill 5 jars full and part of a 6th jar.

B. 15 cc

C. $240 \div 45 = 5$ R15

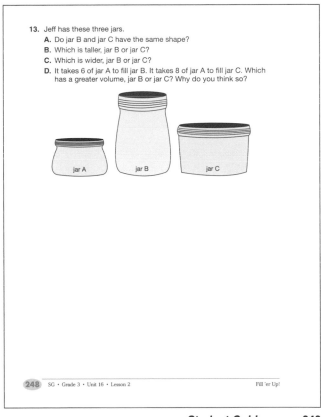

10. Molly fills her 80 cc graduated cylinder with water and empties it into a jar four times. The jar is still not full. She fills the graduated cylinder again. She uses this water to fill the jar to the top. Her graduated cylinder still has 25 cc of water in it. What is the volume of the jar? Show your work.

11. Mimi has a small jar with a volume of 40 cc and a bigger jar with a volume of 230 cc.
   A. How many *full* small jars of water can Mimi pour into her big jar? How much more water does she need to fill the big jar to the top? Show your work.
   B. Write a number sentence for your answer.

12. A container has a volume of 240 cc. You have many small jars, each with a volume of 45 cc. You want to pour all the water from the big container into the small jars.
   A. About how many jars can you fill? First, write down your estimate. Then solve the problem.
   B. How much water will be in the last jar?
   C. Write a division sentence for the problem.

Fill 'er Up!   SG • Grade 3 • Unit 16 • Lesson 2   **247**

Student Guide - page 247

Student Guide (p. 248)

13. A. No

B. jar B

C. jar C

D. jar C; it only takes 6 jar As to fill jar B, but it takes 8 jar As to fill jar C.

13. Jeff has these three jars.
   A. Do jar B and jar C have the same shape?
   B. Which is taller, jar B or jar C?
   C. Which is wider, jar B or jar C?
   D. It takes 6 of jar A to fill jar B. It takes 8 of jar A to fill jar C. Which has a greater volume, jar B or jar C? Why do you think so?

jar A   jar B   jar C

248   SG • Grade 3 • Unit 16 • Lesson 2   Fill 'er Up!

Student Guide - page 248

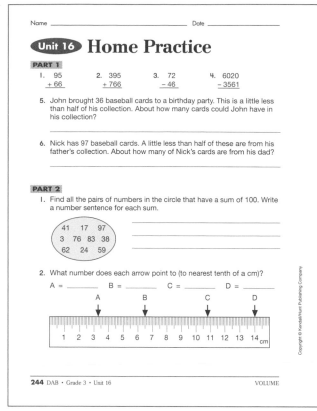

Discovery Assignment Book - page 244

Discovery Assignment Book (p. 244)

Home Practice*

Part 2

1. $97 + 3 = 100$; $83 + 17 = 100$;
   $76 + 24 = 100$; $62 + 38 = 100$;
   $59 + 41 = 100$

2. **A.** 3.3 cm
   B. 6.5 cm
   C. 10.8 cm
   D. 14.0 cm

Name _____ Date _____

PART 3

1. You are given a balance and some 8-gram, 5-gram, and 1-gram masses. How many of each would you need to balance an object with a mass of 78 grams? Show your work.

2. A graduated cylinder is filled with 40 cc of water. Four marbles of the same size are added to the cylinder. The level of the water rises to 52 cc. What is the volume of each marble? Show your work.

3. Tanya's parents told her that if she can save $100.00 towards a new bike, they will pay the rest. So far she has saved $20.00. She makes $9.00 every Saturday baby-sitting. How many weeks will it take Tanya to save $100.00? Show your work.

PART 4

1. How many hops will a +2 mathhopper take to reach or go past 100 if it starts on 0? Show your work on a piece of paper. _____

2. How many hops will a +5 mathhopper need to take to reach 1000 if it starts at 0? Show your work on a piece of paper. _____

3. If a +10 mathhopper starts at 5 and takes 8 hops, on what number will it land? Show your work on a piece of paper. _____

VOLUME   DAB • Grade 3 • Unit 16 **245**

Discovery Assignment Book - page 245

Discovery Assignment Book (p. 245)

Part 3

1. Answers will vary. One possible answer: nine 8-gram masses, one 5-gram mass, and one 1-gram mass

2. 3 cc; $52 \text{ cc} - 40 \text{ cc} = 12 \text{ cc}$;
   $3 \text{ cc} \times 4 \text{ marbles} = 12 \text{ cc}$

3. 9 weeks; $\$100.00 - \$20.00 = \$80.00$;
   9 weeks $\times \$9.00 = \$81.00$ in 9 weeks

*Answers for all the Home Practice in the *Discovery Assignment Book* are at the end of the unit.

Discovery Assignment Book (p. 247)

Volume Hunt

1.–2. Answers will vary.

Name _____ Date _____

Volume Hunt

At Home

1. Find two containers of different sizes: 1 cup, 1 pint, 1 quart, or 1 gallon. Fill the smaller container with water, and empty it into the larger container. How many times can you do this without making the larger container overflow?

2. If your smaller container is a cup, answer Question 2A.
   If your smaller container is a pint, answer Question 2B.
   If your smaller container is a quart, answer Question 2C.

   A. How many cups are in a _____?
      size of larger container

      _____ cups

   B. How many pints are in a _____?
      size of larger container

      _____ pints

   C. How many quarts are in a _____?
      size of larger container

      _____ quarts

Copyright © Kendall/Hunt Publishing Company

Volume Hunt   DAB • Grade 3 • Unit 16 • Lesson 3 **247**

Discovery Assignment Book - page 247

Lesson 3

Volume Hunt

Lesson Overview

Students complete the first part of this lesson at home. They find two containers that have different sizes—a cup, a quart, a pint, or a gallon. The objective of the activity is for students to discover the relationships among these units by pouring water between the different-sized containers. Children then share their results with classmates, record their findings in a data table, and use arithmetic to derive any missing values.

Key Content

- Discovering the relationships among the U.S. Customary Units of Measurement—cup, pint, quart, and gallon.
- Using addition, subtraction, multiplication, and division to solve problems involving volume.

Key Vocabulary

- cup
- gallon
- pint
- quart

Math Facts

Task J provides practice with multiplication facts and money.

Homework

1. *Questions 1–2* of the *Volume Hunt* Activity Pages were assigned at the end of Lesson 2.
2. Assign Part 4 of the Home Practice.

Assessment

Use the *Observational Assessment Record* to document students' abilities to solve addition, subtraction, multiplication, and division problems involving volume.

Materials List

Supplies and Copies

Student	Teacher
Supplies for Each Student • 2 containers of different sizes at home: cup, pint, quart, or gallon **Supplies for Each Student Group** • 1 dishpan or large container • paper towels	**Supplies** • cup, pint, quart, and gallon container
Copies	**Copies/Transparencies** • 1 transparency of *Volume Hunt* data table, optional (*Discovery Assignment Book* Page 248)

All blackline masters including assessment, transparency, and DPP masters are also on the Teacher Resource CD.

Student Books
Volume Hunt (Discovery Assignment Book Pages 247–248)

Daily Practice and Problems and Home Practice
DPP items I–J (*Unit Resource Guide* Pages 16–17)
Home Practice Part 4 (*Discovery Assignment Book* Page 245)

Note: Classrooms whose pacing differs significantly from the suggested pacing of the units should use the Math Facts Calendar in Section 4 of the *Facts Resource Guide* to ensure students receive the complete math facts program.

Assessment Tools
Observational Assessment Record (*Unit Resource Guide* Pages 9–10)

Daily Practice and Problems

Suggestions for using the DPPs are on page 64.

I. Bit: Missing Decimal (URG p. 16)

Find the missing length. Write a number sentence for this problem.

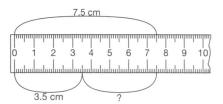

J. Task: Mother's Helpers (URG p. 17)

1. After school, Jan helps her neighbor with her new baby and earns 2 dollars each day. How much does Jan earn if she helps 4 days? 9 days? 7 days? 3 days?

2. Tony helps by going to the store for the neighbor and earns 50 cents each time. How much will Tony earn if he goes to the store 4 times? 5 times? 8 times? 9 times? Write the number sentences.

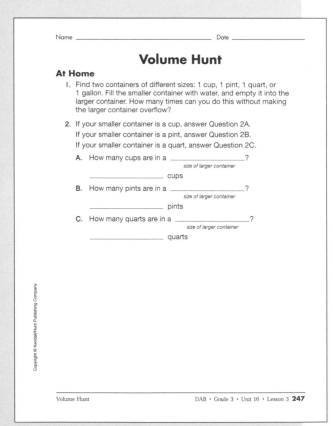

Discovery Assignment Book - page 247 *(Answers on p. 66)*

Before the Activity

Collect examples of cup, pint, quart, and gallon containers for use in class.

Students complete the first page of the *Volume Hunt* Activity Pages in the *Discovery Assignment Book* at home before beginning the lesson in class.

Teaching the Activity

Part 1 Volume Measurements at Home

Discuss with students that although the metric system is used by most scientists, the U.S. Customary System is still frequently used by people in the United States. Explain that in this activity students will discover the relationships between four of the U.S. Customary Units: **the cup, the pint, the quart,** and **the gallon.**

Children begin the activity at home following the directions on the *Volume Hunt* Activity Pages in the *Discovery Assignment Book.* They find two containers of different sizes—a cup, a pint, a quart, or a gallon. For example, they might find pint-sized containers of sour cream or ice cream and quart- or gallon-sized containers of milk and orange juice. Explain that if the students look for a cup at home, they should look for a 1-cup measuring cup, not just any drinking cup. Not every child needs to find every size container.

Next, children fill the smaller container with water and pour it into the larger container. They should count the number of times they can empty the smaller container's water into the larger container without overflowing the larger one. Finally, children analyze their results by answering *Question 2* regarding the relationship between their two containers. They should bring their containers to school and share them with the class.

Part 2 Sharing the Results in Class

Ask students to share their findings from home with the class. Students can share different-sized containers with each other to do more water investigation. *Question 3* directs children to record their data in a table. Record their findings on the transparency of the data table. Make the entries in the unshaded boxes, as shown in Figure 7.

Converting Standard Volume Units

	cup	pint	quart	gallon
number of cups in a	1	2	4	16
number of pints in a		1	2	8
number of quarts in a			1	4
number of gallons in a				1

Figure 7: *Table for converting standard volume units*

If empty boxes still remain after each child has discussed her or his findings, the class may be able to compute the answers from the existing data. For example, if the data shows that there are 2 pints in a quart and 4 quarts in a gallon, children should be able to reason that there are 4×2, or 8, pints in a gallon.

If it is impossible to compute the answers from the existing data because, for instance, no one in the class used a pint container, ask students to look at home to find the specific size containers needed to complete the table. Or have suitable containers available in the classroom. Discuss children's findings in class and complete the table.

TIMS Tip

The containers children find at home may not be precisely the sizes marked on the labels. Although there are four cups in one quart, for example, a container that holds a quart of milk might have extra space for air on top and might hold a little more than four cups. This probably will not be a problem if students round their answers to the nearest whole number.

Name _____ Date _____

In Class
Share your findings with your classmates.

3. Fill in the answers in the unshaded boxes in the table below. You can use arithmetic to help you complete the table.

Converting Standard Volume Units

	cup	pint	quart	gallon
number of cups in a				
number of pints in a				
number of quarts in a				
number of gallons in a				

4. How many cups are in 2 pints? _____
5. How many quarts are in 3 gallons? _____
6. How many cups are in 5 quarts? _____

Copyright © Kendall/Hunt Publishing Company

248 DAB • Grade 3 • Unit 16 • Lesson 3   Volume Hunt

Discovery Assignment Book - page 248 (Answers on p. 67)

Name _____ Date _____

PART 3

1. You are given a balance and some 8-gram, 5-gram, and 1-gram masses. How many of each would you need to balance an object with a mass of 78 grams? Show your work.

_____

2. A graduated cylinder is filled with 40 cc of water. Four marbles of the same size are added to the cylinder. The level of the water rises to 52 cc. What is the volume of each marble? Show your work.

_____

3. Tanya's parents told her that if she can save $100.00 towards a new bike, they will pay the rest. So far she has saved $20.00. She makes $9.00 every Saturday baby-sitting. How many weeks will it take Tanya to save $100.00? Show your work.

_____

_____

PART 4

1. How many hops will a +2 mathhopper take to reach or go past 100 if it starts on 0? Show your work on a piece of paper. _____

2. How many hops will a +5 mathhopper need to take to reach 1000 if it starts at 0? Show your work on a piece of paper. _____

3. If a +10 mathhopper starts at 5 and takes 8 hops, on what number will it land? Show your work on a piece of paper. _____

VOLUME   DAB • Grade 3 • Unit 16 **245**

Discovery Assignment Book - page 245 (Answers on p. 66)

Math Facts

- DPP Task J contains word problems that practice multiplication facts for the twos, fives, and tens in the context of money.

- Home Practice Part 4 contains mathhopper problems that use multiplication facts for the twos, fives, and tens.

Answers for Part 4 of the Home Practice are in the Answer Key at the end of this lesson and at the end of this unit.

Homework and Practice

DPP Bit I provides practice reading a centimeter ruler to the nearest tenth of a centimeter and using the reading to make calculations.

Assessment

Use the *Observational Assessment Record* to note students' abilities to use addition, subtraction, multiplication, and division to solve problems involving volume.

Extension

Challenge students to figure out the answers that go in the shaded boxes of the table. These entries are fractions, as shown in Figure 8.

Converting Standard Volume Units

	cup	pint	quart	gallon
number of cups in a	1	2	4	16
number of pints in a	$\frac{1}{2}$	1	2	8
number of quarts in a	$\frac{1}{4}$	$\frac{1}{2}$	1	4
number of gallons in a	$\frac{1}{16}$	$\frac{1}{8}$	$\frac{1}{4}$	1

Figure 8: *A completed table that includes fractions of units*

At a Glance

Math Facts and Daily Practice and Problems

DPP Bit I involves measuring and calculating in tenths of a centimeter. Task J provides practice with multiplication facts and money.

Part 1. Volume Measurements at Home

1. Discuss with students that in this activity they will find the relationship between four of the U.S. Customary Units for volume: the cup, the pint, the quart, and the gallon.
2. Tell students to find two containers of any of the four sizes at home.
3. Students determine how many times they can fill the smaller container with water and pour it into the larger container. They enter the result on the first *Volume Hunt* Activity Page in the *Discovery Assignment Book.*

Part 2. Sharing the Results in Class

1. Students bring their containers to school to share with each other and collect more data.
2. Students fill in the data table on the *Volume Hunt* Activity Pages.

Homework

1. *Questions 1–2* of the *Volume Hunt* Activity Pages were assigned at the end of Lesson 2.
2. Assign Part 4 of the Home Practice.

Assessment

Use the *Observational Assessment Record* to document students' abilities to solve addition, subtraction, multiplication, and division problems involving volume.

Extension

Challenge students to find the fractional relationships between cups, pints, quarts, and gallons.

Answer Key is on pages 66–67.

Notes:

Name _____ Date _____

PART 3

1. You are given a balance and some 8-gram, 5-gram, and 1-gram masses. How many of each would you need to balance an object with a mass of 78 grams? Show your work.

_____

2. A graduated cylinder is filled with 40 cc of water. Four marbles of the same size are added to the cylinder. The level of the water rises to 52 cc. What is the volume of each marble? Show your work.

_____

3. Tanya's parents told her that if she can save $100.00 towards a new bike, they will pay the rest. So far she has saved $20.00. She makes $9.00 every Saturday baby-sitting. How many weeks will it take Tanya to save $100.00? Show your work.

_____

PART 4

1. How many hops will a +2 mathhopper take to reach or go past 100 if it starts on 0? Show your work on a piece of paper. _____

2. How many hops will a +5 mathhopper need to take to reach 1000 if it starts at 0? Show your work on a piece of paper. _____

3. If a +10 mathhopper starts at 5 and takes 8 hops, on what number will it land? Show your work on a piece of paper. _____

VOLUME   DAB • Grade 3 • Unit 16 **245**

Discovery Assignment Book - page 245

Discovery Assignment Book (p. 245)

Home Practice*

Part 4

1. 50 hops

2. 200 hops

3. 85; $5 + 10 \times 8 = 85$

Name _____ Date _____

Volume Hunt

At Home

1. Find two containers of different sizes: 1 cup, 1 pint, 1 quart, or 1 gallon. Fill the smaller container with water, and empty it into the larger container. How many times can you do this without making the larger container overflow?

2. If your smaller container is a cup, answer Question 2A.
   If your smaller container is a pint, answer Question 2B.
   If your smaller container is a quart, answer Question 2C.

   A. How many cups are in a _____?
                              size of larger container
      _____ cups

   B. How many pints are in a _____?
                              size of larger container
      _____ pints

   C. How many quarts are in a _____?
                               size of larger container
      _____ quarts

Volume Hunt   DAB • Grade 3 • Unit 16 • Lesson 3 **247**

Discovery Assignment Book - page 247

Discovery Assignment Book (p. 247)

Volume Hunt

1.–2. Answers will vary.

---

*Answers for all the Home Practice in the *Discovery Assignment Book* are at the end of the unit.

Discovery Assignment Book (p. 248)

3. See Figure 7 in the Lesson Guide for a completed data table.

4. 4 cups

5. 12 quarts

6. 20 cups

Name _____ Date _____

In Class
Share your findings with your classmates.

3. Fill in the answers in the unshaded boxes in the table below. You can use arithmetic to help you complete the table.

Converting Standard Volume Units

	cup	pint	quart	gallon
number of cups in a				
number of pints in a				
number of quarts in a				
number of gallons in a				

4. How many cups are in 2 pints? _____

5. How many quarts are in 3 gallons? _____

6. How many cups are in 5 quarts? _____

Volume Hunt

Discovery Assignment Book - page 248

Lesson 4

Elixir of Youth

Lesson Overview

Estimated Class Sessions

1

Sam V. and Tess V. Shovel, ace volume investigators, are on a case for the Oriental Museum. Someone has stolen the liquid contents of an ancient jar in the museum's collection and Tess and Sam must find the thief. Through some clever detective work (more than once involving volume measurement), the youthful heroes track the thief to a suspicious dairy barn. The perpetrator is not revealed in the story although a clue is given. Students are invited to write their own endings.

Key Content

- Measuring volume in metric units (cubic centimeters) and customary units (gallons).
- Using multiplication and division to solve problems involving volume.
- Connecting mathematics and social studies.

Key Vocabulary

- elixir
- mileage
- tread
- vase

Math Facts

DPP Bit K is a multiplication quiz on the 2s, 5s, and 10s.

Homework

Assign the word problems in Lesson 5.

Assessment

1. Use DPP Bit K to assess students on the multiplication facts for the 2s, 5s, and 10s.
2. Use DPP Task L to assess students on measuring volume by displacement.
3. Use the *Observational Assessment Record* to note students' abilities to use addition, subtraction, multiplication, and division to solve volume problems.
4. Transfer appropriate documentation from the *Observational Assessment Record* to students' *Individual Assessment Record Sheets.*

Content Note

The Oriental Museum. The Oriental Museum in the story is loosely modeled on the world-famous Oriental Institute on the campus of the University of Chicago. "Oriental," at the time of the Institute's founding, referred to the lands we call the Middle East today.

Supplies and Copies

Student	Teacher
Supplies for Each Student	**Supplies** • map of the Middle East, optional
Copies	**Copies/Transparencies**

All blackline masters including assessment, transparency, and DPP masters are also on the Teacher Resource CD.

Student Books
Elixir of Youth (*Adventure Book* Pages 95–114)

Daily Practice and Problems and Home Practice
DPP items K–L (*Unit Resource Guide* Pages 17–18)

Note: Classrooms whose pacing differs significantly from the suggested pacing of the units should use the Math Facts Calendar in Section 4 of the *Facts Resource Guide* to ensure students receive the complete math facts program.

Assessment Tools
Observational Assessment Record (*Unit Resource Guide* Pages 9–10)
Individual Assessment Record Sheet (*Teacher Implementation Guide,* Assessment section)

Daily Practice and Problems

Suggestions for using the DPPs are on page 76.

Suggestions for using the DPPs are on page 76.

K. Bit: Multiplication Quiz: 2s, 5s, and 10s (URG p. 17)

A. $2 \times 5 =$ B. $5 \times 7 =$ C. $3 \times 10 =$

D. $10 \times 8 =$ E. $8 \times 5 =$ F. $2 \times 7 =$

G. $5 \times 3 =$ H. $4 \times 5 =$ I. $2 \times 8 =$

J. $10 \times 4 =$ K. $9 \times 2 =$ L. $5 \times 5 =$

M. $5 \times 9 =$ N. $10 \times 5 =$ O. $2 \times 6 =$

P. $6 \times 10 =$ Q. $5 \times 6 =$ R. $4 \times 2 =$

S. $10 \times 7 =$ T. $10 \times 2 =$ U. $5 \times 1 =$

V. $4 \times 2 =$ W. $0 \times 2 =$ X. $10 \times 10 =$

Y. $3 \times 2 =$ Z. $10 \times 9 =$

L. Task: Three Marbles (URG p. 18)

A graduated cylinder contains 35 cc of water. Three marbles of the same size are added. The water level rises to 41 cc.

1. Draw two graduated cylinders: one before the marbles are added and one after.
2. What is the volume of each marble?

Adventure Book - page 97

Discussion Prompts

Page 97

- *What modern countries include the regions mentioned (Sumeria, Babylonia, Assyria, and Egypt)?*

Iraq, Kuwait, Iran, Turkey, and Egypt

Page 99

- *How long ago was 685 BC?*

For example: 2008 + 685 = 2693 years ago

Adventure Book - page 99

Page 100

- *If an elephant weighs four tons, about how many elephants would it take to equal 40 tons?*

About 10 elephants

- *If the vase were exactly 4000 years old, then in what year would it have been made?*

One method to solve this is to count back. If the year is 2008, count back 2008 years to 0 BC. Then count back (4000 − 2008) = 1992 years to the year the vase was made.

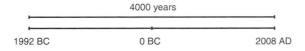

4000 years

1992 BC   0 BC   2008 AD

- *What is an elixir of youth?*

A liquid that restores youth to anyone who drinks it.

Adventure Book - page 100

Adventure Book - page 102

Page 102

- *Have you ever seen a liquid leave a line on the side of a container?*

Answers will vary, but the familiar ring around the bathtub is a good example.

- *What lab are you reminded of by what Sam and Tess are doing? Explain how.*

Fill 'er Up! also involved finding an unknown volume by filling a container with liquid from a container of known volume.

Adventure Book - page 103

Page 103

- *How many gallons are there in 50 buckets if each bucket holds five gallons?*

250 gallons

Page 104

- *How do Sam and Tess know there were 250 milk containers?*

They know because there were 250 gallons of liquid in the vase and each milk container holds one gallon.

Adventure Book - page 104

Page 107

- *Who do you think might be the thief? Why?*

Answers will vary.

Adventure Book - page 107

Adventure Book - page 109

Page 109

- *If Tanya was the last to use the museum station wagon and if she filled it up when she finished, then why is the tank in the station wagon not full now?*

The tank is not full because the thief used the car and didn't fill it up again.

- *How far do you think a car could go on 4 gallons of gas?*

Answers will vary. At 12 miles per gallon, 4 gallons would last 48 miles; at 25 miles per gallon, 100 miles.

Adventure Book - page 110

Page 110

- *How many miles would the museum station wagon go on 2 gallons? On 5 gallons? On 12 gallons?*

40, 100, and 240 miles, respectively

- *How do Sam and Tess know the thief's hideout is about 40 miles away from the museum?*

They figured out that the thief drove a total of 80 miles. Since the thief had to get to the hideout and back again, he or she must have driven 40 miles each way.

Page 111

- *What does the circle on the map show?*

The radius of a circle is the distance from the center to the outside of a circle. The circle indicates all the places that are 40 miles away from the museum in the center of the circle.

Adventure Book - page 111

Page 112

- *Why did Sam say, "That stuff really works!"?*

Sam thought the thief had turned into a baby from drinking the elixir of youth.

- *Is there really any such thing as an elixir of youth?*

No—not yet, anyway.

Adventure Book - page 112

Adventure Book - page 114

Page 114

- *Who do you think the thief is? Explain why you think so.*

Answers will vary. One likely culprit is Howard since the tread on the thief's shoe matches the tread on Howard's shoe. Howard may have wanted to raise money for the museum's Sumerian exhibit.

> ### Journal Prompt
> Write an ending for the story. Tell who the thief is and why he or she committed the robbery.

Homework and Practice

Assign the word problems in Lesson 5 *Paying Taxes Problems* for homework.

Assessment

- DPP Bit K Multiplication Quiz: 2s, 5s, and 10s assesses the multiplication facts in these groups.

- DPP Task L can be used to assess students' understanding of the procedure for measuring volume by displacement.

- Use the *Observational Assessment Record* to note students' abilities to use addition, subtraction, multiplication, and division to solve volume problems.

- Transfer appropriate documentation from the Unit 16 *Observational Assessment Record* to students' *Individual Assessment Record Sheets*.

Extension

Have students write another Sam and Tess volume adventure. You can provide sample titles, such as "The Case of the Disappearing Cider" or "Sam and Tess and Soup for Lunch." Ask them to include lots of volume measuring.

Paying Taxes Problems

Lesson Overview

This lesson is a series of word problems about computing tax. Students interpret a graph and add, subtract, multiply, or divide to solve the problems.

Key Content

- Using patterns in data to solve problems.
- Using addition, subtraction, multiplication, and division to solve problems.
- Solving problems involving money.

Homework

Assign some or all of the problems for homework.

Materials List

Supplies and Copies

Student	Teacher
Supplies for Each Student	**Supplies**
Copies	**Copies/Transparencies**

All blackline masters including assessment, transparency, and DPP masters are also on the Teacher Resource CD.

Student Books

Paying Taxes Problems (*Student Guide* Page 249)

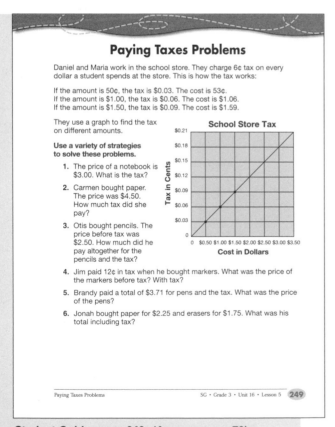

Paying Taxes Problems

Daniel and Maria work in the school store. They charge 6¢ tax on every dollar a student spends at the store. This is how the tax works:

If the amount is 50¢, the tax is $0.03. The cost is 53¢.
If the amount is $1.00, the tax is $0.06. The cost is $1.06.
If the amount is $1.50, the tax is $0.09. The cost is $1.59.

They use a graph to find the tax on different amounts.

Use a variety of strategies to solve these problems.

1. The price of a notebook is $3.00. What is the tax?

2. Carmen bought paper. The price was $4.50. How much tax did she pay?

3. Otis bought pencils. The price before tax was $2.50. How much did he pay altogether for the pencils and the tax?

4. Jim paid 12¢ in tax when he bought markers. What was the price of the markers before tax? With tax?

5. Brandy paid a total of $3.71 for pens and the tax. What was the price of the pens?

6. Jonah bought paper for $2.25 and erasers for $1.75. What was his total including tax?

Paying Taxes Problems   SG • Grade 3 • Unit 16 • Lesson 5 **249**

Student Guide - page 249 *(Answers on p. 79)*

Teaching the Activity

This lesson is another set of word problems that gives students practice analyzing word problems critically and choosing appropriate methods for solving them. The problems in this lesson strengthen computational skills and data analysis. Students use data in a point graph to answer questions about taxes.

Using the Problems. Students can work on the problems individually, in pairs, or in groups. They can work on the problems individually at first and then come together in pairs or small groups to compare solutions. Then the group's solutions can be shared with others in a class discussion. Some or all the problems also can be assigned for homework throughout the unit. Because this activity does not require much teacher preparation, it is appropriate to leave for a substitute teacher.

Homework and Practice

Assign some or all the problems on the *Paying Taxes Problems* Activity Page in the *Student Guide* as homework.

Teaching the Activity

1. Students solve the word problems on the *Paying Taxes Problems* Activity Page in the *Student Guide*.
2. Students discuss solutions and solution strategies.

Homework

Assign some or all the problems for homework.

Notes:

Answer Key • Lesson 5: Paying Taxes Problems

Student Guide (p. 249)

Solution strategies will vary.

1. $0.18
2. $0.27; tax on $3.00 is $0.18. The tax on $1.50 is $0.09. So tax on $4.50 would be $0.27.
3. $2.65; $2.50 + $0.15
4. $2.00; $2.12
5. $3.50; $3.50 + $0.21 = $3.71
6. $4.24

Paying Taxes Problems

Daniel and Maria work in the school store. They charge 6¢ tax on every dollar a student spends at the store. This is how the tax works:

If the amount is 50¢, the tax is $0.03. The cost is 53¢.
If the amount is $1.00, the tax is $0.06. The cost is $1.06.
If the amount is $1.50, the tax is $0.09. The cost is $1.59.

They use a graph to find the tax on different amounts.

Use a variety of strategies to solve these problems.

1. The price of a notebook is $3.00. What is the tax?
2. Carmen bought paper. The price was $4.50. How much tax did she pay?
3. Otis bought pencils. The price before tax was $2.50. How much did he pay altogether for the pencils and the tax?
4. Jim paid 12¢ in tax when he bought markers. What was the price of the markers before tax? With tax?
5. Brandy paid a total of $3.71 for pens and the tax. What was the price of the pens?
6. Jonah bought paper for $2.25 and erasers for $1.75. What was his total including tax?

School Store Tax

(graph: Tax in Cents vs Cost in Dollars)

Paying Taxes Problems   SG • Grade 3 • Unit 16 • Lesson 5   **249**

Student Guide - page 249

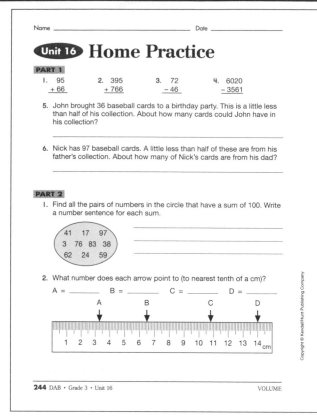

Discovery Assignment Book - page 244

Discovery Assignment Book (p. 244)

Home Practice

Part 1

1. 161
2. 1161
3. 26
4. 2459
5. about 73–80 cards
6. about 45–48 cards

Part 2

1. $97 + 3 = 100$; $83 + 17 = 100$;
   $76 + 24 = 100$; $62 + 38 = 100$;
   $59 + 41 = 100$

2. A. 3.3 cm
   B. 6.5 cm
   C. 10.8 cm
   D. 14.0 cm

Name _____ **Date** _____

PART 3

1. You are given a balance and some 8-gram, 5-gram, and 1-gram masses. How many of each would you need to balance an object with a mass of 78 grams? Show your work.

2. A graduated cylinder is filled with 40 cc of water. Four marbles of the same size are added to the cylinder. The level of the water rises to 52 cc. What is the volume of each marble? Show your work.

3. Tanya's parents told her that if she can save $100.00 towards a new bike, they will pay the rest. So far she has saved $20.00. She makes $9.00 every Saturday baby-sitting. How many weeks will it take Tanya to save $100.00? Show your work.

PART 4

1. How many hops will a +2 mathhopper take to reach or go past 100 if it starts on 0? Show your work on a piece of paper. _____

2. How many hops will a +5 mathhopper need to take to reach 1000 if it starts at 0? Show your work on a piece of paper. _____

3. If a +10 mathhopper starts at 5 and takes 8 hops, on what number will it land? Show your work on a piece of paper. _____

Discovery Assignment Book - page 245

Discovery Assignment Book (p. 245)

Part 3

1. Answers will vary. One possible answer: nine 8-gram masses, one 5-gram mass, and one 1-gram mass

2. 3 cc; $52\ cc - 40\ cc = 12\ cc$;
   $3\ cc \times 4\ marbles = 12\ cc$

3. 9 weeks; $\$100.00 - \$20.00 = \$80.00$;
   9 weeks $\times \$9.00 = \$81.00$ in 9 weeks

Part 4

1. 50 hops
2. 200 hops
3. 85; $5 + 10 \times 8 = 85$

Glossary

This glossary provides definitions of key vocabulary terms in the Grade 3 lessons. Locations of key vocabulary terms in the curriculum are included with each definition. Components Key: URG = *Unit Resource Guide,* SG = *Student Guide,* and DAB = *Discovery Assignment Book.*

A

Area (URG Unit 5; SG Unit 5)
The area of a shape is the amount of space it covers, measured in square units.

Array (URG Unit 7 & Unit 11)
An array is an arrangement of elements into a rectangular pattern of (horizontal) rows and (vertical) columns. (*See* column and row.)

Associative Property of Addition (URG Unit 2)
For any three numbers $a, b,$ and c we have $a + (b + c) = (a + b) + c$. For example in finding the sum of 4, 8, and 2, one can compute $4 + 8$ first and then add 2: $(4 + 8) + 2 = 14$. Alternatively, we can compute $8 + 2$ and then add the result to 4: $4 + (8 + 2) = 4 + 10 = 14$.

Average (URG Unit 5)
A number that can be used to represent a typical value in a set of data. (*See also* mean and median.)

Axes (URG Unit 8; SG Unit 8)
Reference lines on a graph. In the Cartesian coordinate system, the axes are two perpendicular lines that meet at the origin. The singular of axes is axis.

B

Base (of a cube model) (URG Unit 18; SG Unit 18)
The part of a cube model that sits on the "ground."

Base-Ten Board (URG Unit 4)
A tool to help children organize base-ten pieces when they are representing numbers.

Base-Ten Pieces (URG Unit 4; SG Unit 4)
A set of manipulatives used to model our number system as shown in the figure at the right. Note that a skinny is made of 10 bits, a flat is made of 100 bits, and a pack is made of 1000 bits.

Base-Ten Shorthand (SG Unit 4)
A pictorial representation of the base-ten pieces as shown.

Nickname	Picture	Shorthand
bit	▱	•
skinny	▭▭▭▭▭	/
flat		◻
pack		◻

Best-Fit Line (URG Unit 9; SG Unit 9; DAB Unit 9)
The line that comes closest to the most number of points on a point graph.

Bit (URG Unit 4; SG Unit 4)
A cube that measures 1 cm on each edge. It is the smallest of the base-ten pieces that is often used to represent 1. (*See also* base-ten pieces.)

C

Capacity (URG Unit 16)
1. The volume of the inside of a container.
2. The largest volume a container can hold.

Cartesian Coordinate System (URG Unit 8)
A method of locating points on a flat surface by means of numbers. This method is named after its originator, René Descartes. (*See also* coordinates.)

Centimeter (cm)
A unit of measure in the metric system equal to one-hundredth of a meter. (1 inch = 2.54 cm)

Column (URG Unit 11)
In an array, the objects lined up vertically.

Common Fraction (URG Unit 15)
Any fraction that is written with a numerator and denominator that are whole numbers. For example, $\frac{3}{4}$ and $\frac{9}{4}$ are both common fractions. (*See also* decimal fraction.)

Commutative Property of Addition (URG Unit 2 & Unit 11)
This is also known as the Order Property of Addition. Changing the order of the addends does not change the sum. For example, $3 + 5 = 5 + 3 = 8$. Using variables, $n + m = m + n$.

Commutative Property of Multiplication (URG Unit 11)
Changing the order of the factors in a multiplication problem does not change the result, e.g., $7 \times 3 = 3 \times 7 = 21$. (*See also* turn-around facts.)

Congruent (URG Unit 12 & Unit 17; SG Unit 12)
Figures with the same shape and size.

Convenient Number (URG Unit 6)
A number used in computation that is close enough to give a good estimate, but is also easy to compute mentally, e.g., 25 and 30 are convenient numbers for 27.

Coordinates (URG Unit 8; SG Unit 8)
An ordered pair of numbers that locates points on a flat surface by giving distances from a pair of coordinate axes. For example, if a point has coordinates (4, 5) it is 4 units from the vertical axis and 5 units from the horizontal axis.

Counting Back (URG Unit 2)
A strategy for subtracting in which students start from a larger number and then count down until the number is reached. For example, to solve $8 - 3$, begin with 8 and count down three, 7, 6, 5.

Counting Down (*See* counting back.)

Counting Up (URG Unit 2)
A strategy for subtraction in which the student starts at the lower number and counts on to the higher number. For example, to solve $8 - 5$, the student starts at 5 and counts up three numbers (6, 7, 8). So $8 - 5 = 3$.

Cube (SG Unit 18)
A three-dimensional shape with six congruent square faces.

Cubic Centimeter (cc) (URG Unit 16; SG Unit 16)
The volume of a cube that is one centimeter long on each edge.

cubic centimeter

Cup (URG Unit 16)
A unit of volume equal to 8 fluid ounces, one-half pint.

D

Decimal Fraction (URG Unit 15)
A fraction written as a decimal. For example, 0.75 and 0.4 are decimal fractions and $\frac{75}{100}$ and $\frac{4}{10}$ are called common fractions. (*See also* fraction.)

Denominator (URG Unit 13)
The number below the line in a fraction. The denominator indicates the number of equal parts in which the unit whole is divided. For example, the 5 is the denominator in the fraction $\frac{2}{5}$. In this case the unit whole is divided into five equal parts.

Density (URG Unit 16)
The ratio of an object's mass to its volume.

Difference (URG Unit 2)
The answer to a subtraction problem.

Dissection (URG Unit 12 & Unit 17)
Cutting or decomposing a geometric shape into smaller shapes that cover it exactly.

Distributive Property of Multiplication over Addition (URG Unit 19)
For any three numbers *a, b,* and *c, a* $\times$ *(b + c)* = *a* $\times$ *b* + *a* $\times$ *c.* The distributive property is the foundation for most methods of multidigit multiplication. For example, $9 \times (17) = 9 \times (10 + 7) = 9 \times 10 + 9 \times 7 = 90 + 63 = 153$.

E

Equal-Arm Balance
See two-pan balance.

Equilateral Triangle (URG Unit 7)
A triangle with all sides of equal length and all angles of equal measure.

Equivalent Fractions (SG Unit 17)
Fractions that have the same value, e.g., $\frac{2}{4} = \frac{1}{2}$.

Estimate (URG Unit 5 & Unit 6)
1. (verb) To find *about* how many.
2. (noun) An approximate number.

Extrapolation (URG Unit 7)
Using patterns in data to make predictions or to estimate values that lie beyond the range of values in the set of data.

F

Fact Family (URG Unit 11; SG Unit 11)
Related math facts, e.g., $3 \times 4 = 12$, $4 \times 3 = 12$, $12 \div 3 = 4$, $12 \div 4 = 3$.

Factor (URG Unit 11; SG Unit 11)
1. In a multiplication problem, the numbers that are multiplied together. In the problem $3 \times 4 = 12$, 3 and 4 are the factors.
2. Whole numbers that can be multiplied together to get a number. That is, numbers that divide a number evenly, e.g., 1, 2, 3, 4, 6, and 12 are all the factors of 12.

Fewest Pieces Rule (URG Unit 4 & Unit 6; SG Unit 4)
Using the least number of base-ten pieces to represent a number. (*See also* base-ten pieces.)

Flat (URG Unit 4; SG Unit 4)
A block that measures 1 cm $\times$ 10 cm $\times$ 10 cm. It is one of the base-ten pieces that is often used to represent 100. (*See also* base-ten pieces.)

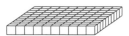

Flip (URG Unit 12)
A motion of the plane in which a figure is reflected over a line so that any point and its image are the same distance from the line.

Fraction (URG Unit 15)
A number that can be written as $\frac{a}{b}$ where a and b are whole numbers and b is not zero. For example, $\frac{1}{2}$, 0.5, and 2 are all fractions since 0.5 can be written as $\frac{5}{10}$ and 2 can be written as $\frac{2}{1}$.

Front-End Estimation (URG Unit 6)
Estimation by looking at the left-most digit.

G

Gallon (gal) (URG Unit 16)
A unit of volume equal to four quarts.

Gram
The basic unit used to measure mass.

H

Hexagon (SG Unit 12)
A six-sided polygon.

Horizontal Axis (SG Unit 1)
In a coordinate grid, the *x*-axis. The axis that extends from left to right.

I

Interpolation (URG Unit 7)
Making predictions or estimating values that lie between data points in a set of data.

J

K

Kilogram
1000 grams.

L

Likely Event (SG Unit 1)
An event that has a high probability of occurring.

Line of Symmetry (URG Unit 12)
A line is a line of symmetry for a plane figure if, when the figure is folded along this line, the two parts match exactly.

Line Symmetry (URG Unit 12; SG Unit 12)
A figure has line symmetry if it has at least one line of symmetry.

Liter (l) (URG Unit 16; SG Unit 16)
Metric unit used to measure volume. A liter is a little more than a quart.

M

Magic Square (URG Unit 2)
A square array of digits in which the sums of the rows, columns, and main diagonals are the same.

Making a Ten (URG Unit 2)
Strategies for addition and subtraction that make use of knowing the sums to ten. For example, knowing $6 + 4 = 10$ can be helpful in finding $10 - 6 = 4$ and $11 - 6 = 5$.

Mass (URG Unit 9 & Unit 16; SG Unit 9)
The amount of matter in an object.

Mean (URG Unit 5)
An average of a set of numbers that is found by adding the values of the data and dividing by the number of values.

Measurement Division (URG Unit 7)
Division as equal grouping. The total number of objects and the number of objects in each group are known. The number of groups is the unknown. For example, tulip bulbs come in packages of 8. If 216 bulbs are sold, how many packages are sold?

Measurement Error (URG Unit 9)
The unavoidable error that occurs due to the limitations inherent to any measurement instrument.

Median (URG Unit 5; DAB Unit 5)
For a set with an odd number of data arranged in order, it is the middle number. For an even number of data arranged in order, it is the number halfway between the two middle numbers.

Meniscus (URG Unit 16; SG Unit 16)
The curved surface formed when a liquid creeps up the side of a container (for example, a graduated cylinder).

Meter (m)
The standard unit of length measure in the metric system. One meter is approximately 39 inches.

Milliliter (ml) (URG Unit 16; SG Unit 16)
A measure of capacity in the metric system that is the volume of a cube that is one centimeter long on each edge.

Multiple (URG Unit 3 & Unit 11)
A number is a multiple of another number if it is evenly divisible by that number. For example, 12 is a multiple of 2 since 2 divides 12 evenly.

N

Numerator (URG Unit 13)
The number written above the line in a fraction. For example, the 2 is the numerator in the fraction $\frac{2}{5}$. (*See also* denominator.)

O

One-Dimensional Object (URG Unit 18; SG Unit 18)
An object is one-dimensional if it is made up of pieces of lines and curves.

Ordered Pairs (URG Unit 8)
A pair of numbers that gives the coordinates of a point on a grid in relation to the origin. The horizontal coordinate is given first; the vertical coordinate is given second. For example, the ordered pair (5, 3) tells us to move five units to the right of the origin and 3 units up.

Origin (URG Unit 8)
The point at which the *x*- and *y*-axes (horizontal and vertical axes) intersect on a coordinate plane. The origin is described by the ordered pair (0, 0) and serves as a reference point so that all the points on the plane can be located by ordered pairs.

P

Pack (URG Unit 4; SG Unit 4)
A cube that measures 10 cm on each edge. It is one of the base-ten pieces that is often used to represent 1000. (*See also* base-ten pieces.)

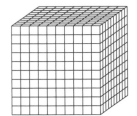

Palindrome (URG Unit 6)
A number, word, or phrase that reads the same forward and backward, e.g., 12321.

Parallel Lines (URG Unit 18)
Lines that are in the same direction. In the plane, parallel lines are lines that do not intersect.

Parallelogram (URG Unit 18)
A quadrilateral with two pairs of parallel sides.

Partitive Division (URG Unit 7)
Division as equal sharing. The total number of objects and the number of groups are known. The number of objects in each group is the unknown. For example, Frank has 144 marbles that he divides equally into 6 groups. How many marbles are in each group?

Pentagon (SG Unit 12)
A five-sided, five-angled polygon.

Perimeter (URG Unit 7; DAB Unit 7)
The distance around a two-dimensional shape.

Pint (URG Unit 16)
A unit of volume measure equal to 16 fluid ounces, i.e., two cups.

Polygon
A two-dimensional connected figure made of line segments in which each endpoint of every side meets with an endpoint of exactly one other side.

Population (URG Unit 1; SG Unit 1)
A collection of persons or things whose properties will be analyzed in a survey or experiment.

Prediction (SG Unit 1)
Using data to declare or foretell what is likely to occur.

Prime Number (URG Unit 11)
A number that has exactly two factors. For example, 7 has exactly two distinct factors, 1 and 7.

Prism
A three-dimensional figure that has two congruent faces, called bases, that are parallel to each other, and all other faces are parallelograms.

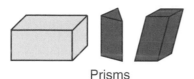

Prisms   Not a prism

Product (URG Unit 11; SG Unit 11; DAB Unit 11)
The answer to a multiplication problem. In the problem $3 \times 4 = 12$, 12 is the product.

Q

Quadrilateral (URG Unit 18)
A polygon with four sides.

Quart (URG Unit 16)
A unit of volume equal to 32 fluid ounces; one quarter of a gallon.

R

Recording Sheet (URG Unit 4)
A place value chart used for addition and subtraction problems.

Rectangular Prism (URG Unit 18; SG Unit 18)
A prism whose bases are rectangles. A right rectangular prism is a prism having all faces rectangles.

Regular (URG Unit 7; DAB Unit 7)
A polygon is regular if all sides are of equal length and all angles are equal.

Remainder (URG Unit 7)
Something that remains or is left after a division problem. The portion of the dividend that is not evenly divisible by the divisor, e.g., $16 \div 5 = 3$ with 1 as a remainder.

Right Angle (SG Unit 12)
An angle that measures 90°.

Rotation (turn) (URG Unit 12)
A transformation (motion) in which a figure is turned a specified angle and direction around a point.

Row (URG Unit 11)
In an array, the objects lined up horizontally.

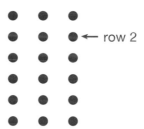
← row 2

Rubric (URG Unit 2)
A written guideline for assigning scores to student work, for the purpose of assessment.

S

Sample (URG Unit 1; SG Unit 1)
A part or subset of a population.

Skinny (URG Unit 4; SG Unit 4)
A block that measures 1 cm $\times$ 1 cm $\times$ 10 cm. It is one of the base-ten pieces that is often used to represent 10. (*See also* base-ten pieces.)

Square Centimeter (sq cm) (SG Unit 5)
The area of a square that is 1 cm long on each side.

Square Number (SG Unit 11)
A number that is the product of a whole number multiplied by itself. For example, 25 is a square number since $5 \times 5 = 25$. A square number can be represented by a square array with the same number of rows as columns. A square array for 25 has 5 rows of 5 objects in each row or 25 total objects.

Standard Masses
A set of objects with convenient masses, usually 1 g, 10 g, 100 g, etc.

Sum (URG Unit 2; SG Unit 2)
The answer to an addition problem.

Survey (URG Unit 14; SG Unit 14)
An investigation conducted by collecting data from a sample of a population and then analyzing it. Usually surveys are used to make predictions about the entire population.

T

Tangrams (SG Unit 12)
A type of geometric puzzle. A shape is given and it must be covered exactly with seven standard shapes called tans.

Thinking Addition (URG Unit 2)
A strategy for subtraction that uses a related addition problem. For example, $15 - 7 = 8$ because $8 + 7 = 15$.

Three-Dimensional (URG Unit 18; SG Unit 18)
Existing in three-dimensional space; having length, width, and depth.

TIMS Laboratory Method (URG Unit 1; SG Unit 1)
A method that students use to organize experiments and investigations. It involves four components: draw, collect, graph, and explore. It is a way to help students learn about the scientific method.

Turn (URG Unit 12)
(*See* rotation.)

Turn-Around Facts (URG Unit 2 & Unit 11 p. 37; SG Unit 11)
Addition facts that have the same addends but in a different order, e.g., $3 + 4 = 7$ and $4 + 3 = 7$. (*See also* commutative property of addition and commutative property of multiplication.)

Two-Dimensional (URG Unit 18; SG Unit 18)
Existing in the plane; having length and width.

Two-Pan Balance
A device for measuring the mass of an object by balancing the object against a number of standard masses (usually multiples of 1 unit, 10 units, and 100 units, etc.).

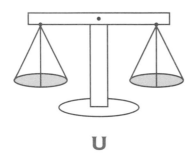

U

Unit (of measurement) (URG Unit 18)
A precisely fixed quantity used to measure. For example, centimeter, foot, kilogram, and quart are units of measurement.

Using a Ten (URG Unit 2)
1. A strategy for addition that uses partitions of the number 10. For example, one can find $8 + 6$ by thinking $8 + 6 = 8 + 2 + 4 = 10 + 4 = 14$.
2. A strategy for subtraction that uses facts that involve subtracting 10. For example, students can use $17 - 10 = 7$ to learn the "close fact" $17 - 9 = 8$.

Using Doubles (URG Unit 2)
Strategies for addition and subtraction that use knowing doubles. For example, one can find $7 + 8$ by thinking $7 + 8 = 7 + 7 + 1 = 14 + 1 = 15$. Knowing $7 + 7 = 14$ can be helpful in finding $14 - 7 = 7$ and $14 - 8 = 6$.

V

Value (URG Unit 1; SG Unit 1)
The possible outcomes of a variable. For example, red, green, and blue are possible values for the variable *color*. Two meters and 1.65 meters are possible values for the variable *length*.

Variable (URG Unit 1; SG Unit 1)
1. An attribute or quantity that changes or varies.
2. A symbol that can stand for a variable.

Vertex (URG Unit 12; SG Unit 12)
1. A point where the sides of a polygon meet.
2. A point where the edges of a three-dimensional object meet.

Vertical Axis (SG Unit 1)
In a coordinate grid, the y-axis. It is perpendicular to the horizontal axis.

Volume (URG Unit 16; SG Unit 16)
The measure of the amount of space occupied by an object.

Volume by Displacement (URG Unit 16)
A way of measuring volume of an object by measuring the amount of water (or some other fluid) it displaces.

W

Weight (URG Unit 9)
A measure of the pull of gravity on an object. One unit for measuring weight is the pound.

X

Y

Z